On a Barge in France

Harvey Schwartz

ISBN: 978-0-692-62474-6

Thank you to the people of France, who opened their homes, their hearts and even their canal locks to us as we wandered through their country.

And thank you, of course, to the Queen of the forward deck.

Hoop Doet Leven

Contents

France

Four French soldiers, my neighbors from the 511th Regiment du Train of the Armée de Terre, stood in line at the ATM across from the Pharmacie Napoleon. Jungle camouflage uniforms. Pants tucked into shiny black boots. Itsy bitsy teeny weeny black berets glued to their foreheads at belligerent angles. They murmured militantly among themselves. An officer marched up. The first soldier saluted. The officer saluted back. The second soldier shook hands. The officer shook hands back. The third soldier placed both hands on the officer's shoulders and kissed him on both cheeks. The officer kissed the soldier's cheeks in return. The fourth soldier checked his iPhone for email.

The officer took his place at the end of the line, waiting to withdraw weekend cash.

I stood in the pharmacy doorway. Shook my head in astonishment.

Four years in France and I haven't a clue how this country works, I thought. Then I walked to the Boulangerie Simone, my favorite of the four bakeries in my winter home of Auxonne, in rural Burgundy, silently practicing how I would ask for two pain au chocolates and one baguette, knowing I would mangle my pronunciation of as simple a word as "one," saying "un" or "oon" or "ah-oon" or "ahn" or some other not-to-be-understood collection of moans and murmurs. More likely I would throw in the towel on even elementary French and, as I usually did, ask for two - deux - loaves of bread, just as I had on hundreds of morning visits to boulangeries across France.

The freezer on my boat, Hoop Doet Leven, was stuffed with frozen corpses of second baguettes I'd purchased.

I was living the retirement dream. Move to France. Buy an old canal barge. Travel the countryside. Eat snails. Drink wine. Live life without a care.

Live life without a clue was more like it.

Lafayette, we are here

Buy an old canal barge in France.

That was our daydream. Then a possibility, my alternative to learning golf in retirement.

Here is how it became our reality.

"Jean Claude" was our first encounter with a genuine French barge guy. (WARNING: please check out the Editorial Note at the end of this chapter.) After my wife Sandra and I sorted, arranged and rearranged, analyzed and categorized, backed up, copied and merged Excel spread-sheets of canal barges for sale in France, all of which we'd discovered by pouring the internet through electronic sieves and filters so that only the absolutely perfect boat would be revealed, it was time for the next step. We flew to France. Properly. On Air France. With visions of in-flight quiche, Chablis and pain au chocolate. We were initiated into the mystery of all-things-France at the Air France ticket counter at Boston's Logan Airport with the first of a thousand permutations of "no-no-no, that is not possible." It turned out that while the web site we'd purchased our tickets from said Air France at the top and our tickets said Air France at both the top and bottom, Air France itself, meaning long winged objects with "Air France" painted on their sides, didn't actually fly from Boston to Paris at that time. No, no, no, monsieur and madame, you must go to the Delta counter. At the Delta terminal. At the other end of the airport. Maybe not actually in Boston itself.

Have a nice flight.

So we flew to France on a plane that said Delta on the side. No quiche. Burgers. Microwaved hamburgers. But our rental Renault at Charles De Gaulle Airport in Paris had a clever TomTom GPS unit stuck to the inside of the windshield, directing us in a saucy female voice with just a hint, from her mother perhaps or, more likely, from her childhood nursemaid, of, could it be, a French accent. Mimi, we called her. Days before takeoff I'd downloaded a GPS app with a French highway map to my iPad, as an experiment. The iPad app was British, most likely having presented an opportunity for Jim Carter to pick up a few quid as a voice model during the off season from playing Carson the Butler on Downton Abbey. We were doubly directed by Mimi and Carson through our first French driving experience. How fortunate. And safe. A guiding angel on each shoulder.

How complacent we were, as we learned shortly after cruising onto the highway.

Take the first exit at the roundabout, Mimi cooed.

What did you just say, Carson screamed. Not the first exit. Take the third exit.

No, the first, Mimi retorted, a slight huff to her voice.

This woman is a fool, Carson told us, an electronic chill in his haughty tone. Ignore her every word if you know whats good for you.

A sound like, yes, a sob from the TomTom unit.

Followed by silence. Was Mimi sulking, or had Sandra, fed up with our introduction to the chill that fails to warm interactions between the French and the British, pulled Mimi's plug?

Five hours later Carson had led us south from Paris into the depths of Bourgogne, which is what the French – correctly, after all, it is their country – call Burgundy. We didn't know it, but we'd spend the better part of the next year in Bourgogne, swearing our loyalty to Burgundy wine, refusing to even brush our teeth with that red swill from arch rival Bordeaux. We couldn't have been more loyal to the Boston Red Sox or scornful of those spawns of the devil himself, the arrogant New York Yankees.

4

We were at St. Jean-des-Losne, the self-declared barge capital of France, at the confluence of the Canal de Bourgogne, the Canal du Rhine au Rhone and the River Saone. In olden days commercial barges used to hang out at St. Jean waiting for cargo. Now, it is stuffed to the gills with self-drive rental boats on which gaggles of people who have never before been on a boat spend week-long vacations bumping into each other. We went there first because it is also the elephant burial ground for used barges, the place where people who have had their fill of floating through France bring their boats to sell them to people – like us – setting sail on their lifelong dreams, or a reasonable facsimile thereof.

In a lifetime of sailing, I've bought and sold half a dozen boats, mostly old boats. Old wooden boats. Mostly beautiful boats since, as people who buy leaky old wood boats comfort one another, life is too short to sail an ugly boat. I'm familiar with the malady that makes the buying and selling of old boats possible: a chronic disease called boat lust. Boat lust is what blinds the buyer's vision as he inspects the Most Beautiful Vessel Ever to Float (or not float). I've had boat lust. I've witnessed boat lust in a man who once bought a wood boat from me as he actually pushed his hand through the rotted wood hull planking, then turned to me and stated, as if it were true, "now that isn't a serious problem, right."

Boat lust. It's a beautiful, treacherous thing.

We drove to St. Jean des Losne in passionate anticipation of seeing our first in the flesh, or in the iron, canal barge. We were infected with a bad case of boat lust, French version.

Which brought us to Jean Claude's door. Jean Claude ran a business providing moorings, storage, maintenance, repairs, oversight and brokerage for several dozen barges. Jean Claude was "the best," we'd read on several barge web sites. We knocked on the door of the former mill, or at least the half of the stone mill building still covered by a roof, that Jean Claude used as his office.

He opened the door and we were charmed.

Jean Claude was the Frenchman provided by Central Casting when the movie script says, "The door was opened by a French man, stringy hair to his shoulders, a cigarette permanently attached to his lower lip, wearing the bulky sweater he'd put on three weeks earlier and not yet taken off. He is charming."

5

"Jean Claude," I said, knowing from our months of back and forth emails about barges he listed for sale at his marina that he spoke English. Sandra and I had practiced saying "Jean Claude" at home. We didn't want to embarrass ourselves at our first meeting. I carefully said "Jean" using the Frenchified "J" sound, like the "s" in pleasure or treasure rather than an American "g", like in "I dream of Jeanne." I dragged it out, to emphasize my sophistication.

"D-ja-ah-ean Claude. I'm Harvey. This is Sandra. It is wonderful to finally meet you after all the emails we've exchanged. I feel as if I know you."

Sandra joined in. "We've been so excited about meeting you and seeing some barges."

The appointment with Jean Claude had been on our kitchen calendar, in red magic marker, highlighted in yellow highlighter, red, white and blue arrows spanning surrounding dates pointed at MEETING WITH JEAN CLAUDE!!!! Red and green balloons were pasted to the calendar. Breakfast conversations at home started with "only two weeks until our meeting with Jean Claude to look at barges."

Jean Claude stood in the doorway. He looked down at his feet, thinking. He looked up.

"Tell me, monsieur, madame. Who did you say you are? Do I know you? And why are you here?"

Evidently, Jean Claude's calendar had no "Harvey and Sandra" in magic marker, highlighted in yellow. Or any other color. He looked at his watch.

"This is a very busy day," he said. "Is it possible for you to come back some other time? Tomorrow, perhaps?" He shook his head. "No, not tomorrow. Tomorrow I have lunch in Chalon-sur-Saone. Next week?"

I heard balloons popping. Red ones. Green ones.

We were patient. We did not get upset. At least we did not show how upset we were. Who would not be disappointed? We'd just learned there was no Santa Claus. No tooth fairy. No Easter Bunny (they eat the Easter Bunny in France, but learning that, in fact, learning to enjoy lapin for lunch came later, during Advanced Life in France 102). Jean Claude had no idea who we were.

Patience paid off. Things worked out. Jean Claude invited us in. We sat in his office. We talked. He talked. He made coffee for us. Showed us photos of his daughter. His dog. His friends. His parents. His house. Paris. Some random mountains. Eventually, meaning after three hours, he ran out of photos. And coffee. And things to talk about. Things that had yet to include any mention of barges. We'd arrived at 9:00 a.m.. I was about to attempt to raise what I suspected was a delicate topic to raise with a French boat broker, the question of whether we might actually see any of the dozen barges he'd listed for sale on his web site. But he beat me to the punch.

He looked at his watch in shocked surprise. "Oh, I am sorry."

Jean Claude shot to his feet. Sandra and I stood, too, excited about finally getting to see a barge.

"Lunch," Jean Claude declared. "Can you come back at 2:00. No, better 2:30." And he walked out the door. We found a restaurant in St. Jean des Losne for the first of what would be years of two-hour lunches.

We returned at precisely 2:30 – 14:30 in the 24-hour time used universally, except not always, in France – and found the office door locked. At 3:00 – 15:00 as we would learn to call 3:00 o'clock in the afternoon – Jean Claude showed up in his Citroen. "Would you like to look at a boat," he asked.

Before we could reply, his phone rang, playing, what else, La Marseillaise. How perfect.

"Oui. Oui. Oui," he said into the phone. "Certainement. Pas de problème. Immédiatement. I will take care of everything."

The phone returned to his desk. "My best client," he told us. "His boat's engine just died. Smoke all over the engine room. He is marooned, marooned in Alsace.

"Did I tell you, this man is my best client. I service his barge throughout France."

We returned to the office. He made coffee for us. Did I show you the photos of my daughter's school trip to Germany? Oui? More cafe?

The office phone rang.

"Oui. Oui. Oui. Un moment." Jean Claude put the caller on hold, placing the phone's handset on the desk. "My client again. The fire is almost out. He is tied to a tree on the side of the canal."

Well, that was certainly good news. Then, without missing a beat, Jean Claude continued his morning dialogue.

"At lunch my daughter told me about her school trip to Berlin. I went to Germany three years ago. I confess, it was an interesting country. But French beer is better."

"Do you speak German," Sandra asked, glancing guiltily at the telephone handset on the desk and the blinking "hold" light on the telephone.

"No, not a word of German," Jean Claude replied. "I should learn German. I have a few German clients. But I already speak the most beautiful language in the world. French is like music, don't you agree. It does not make sense to learn a less beautiful language."

I'd had enough. We'd been at this since 9:00 a.m. It was mid-afternoon. I screwed up my courage.

"Is it possible to see one of the barges you list on your web site for sale," I demanded, trying my best to hide the desperation I was feeling.

Jean Claude took this demand in stride. The French word "demande" is not as formidable as its English equivalent. To "demande" in French is to simply request, an expression of your wish, your slightest preference. My "demande" to see a barge could have been a whim, a passing fancy, not much more than a random thought that had just entered my mind. No need to mention the calendar at home, the magic marker. The highlighting. The circles. Arrows. Balloons.

"But of course," Jean Claude replied, agreeing that showing us a barge we might be interested in buying from him was a splendid concept. "Is there any particular boat I can show you?"

Voila. Finally. Months of anticipation. Hour after hour on the internet. Trading emails with discoveries of could-this-be-our-barge photos and listings and details about engine horsepower and water tank capacity. Emails with Jean Claude requesting detailed specification sheets on the boats he listed. We were going to see our first barge. In France. The countdown to blastoff for our new lives was about to begin.

Start with our number one candidate, I decided. Why not?

"How about ANGELINE, the 24 meter Luxemotor in perfect condition? Let's start with that boat," I said.

"No. You don't want a Luxemotor," Jean Claude replied, not a hint of doubt in his authoritative voice. "They have pointy bows. Luxemotors go straight where you point them. They are too easy to steer.

"You would be bored with a Luxemotor. You should buy a tjalk." He pronounced it as "chalk," like what your third grade teacher used to write with on the blackboard. "A tjalk is beautifully round at the bow, like a wooden Dutch shoe. Very difficult to handle. Especially entering a canal lock. Impossible if there is any wind. Frightening in the wind. Cannot be handled in the wind.

"You won't be bored in a tjalk." He laughed. "Would you like to see a tjalk?"

Sandra glared at me. She knew all about "boat" and "frightening" being good buddies of one another. I'd promised her that "barge" and "frightening" had never met.

But Jean Claude had a point. Tjalks were pretty. In a funky, Dutch clog kind of way. There was a tjalk on his web site that was interesting. With a big kitchen. And a bath tub. Sandra actually thought we could get a barge with a bath tub, back in those days of our innocence.

"What about AUNT MARIE," I asked. "Let's take a look at that tjalk, at least for starters."

"She is a beautiful boat," Jean Claude agreed. "In fantastic condition. The engine was just serviced. The hull was painted last year. And the owner is anxious to sell. Would you like to see AUNT MARIE?"

Sandra and I looked at each other. AUNT MARIE was high on our list, from before we'd been told that tjalks were "interesting" to handle. She nodded.

"Sure," I said. "Lets look at her." I stood up. Sandra stood up.

"I think she's in Belgium." Jean Claude mumbled. "Or maybe Holland. They're cruising until November.

"Come. We'll see if we can find them."

He stood, car keys in hand.

I sat down. Sandra sat down. Neither of us wanted to launch an expedition to Belgium "or maybe Holland." I'd try something else, I thought.

"Let's see AVENTURE instead," I said, adding, before Jean Claude could say anything, "I know it's a Luxemotor with a pointy bow but to tell the truth we've never been on any barge and we really, really want to see one today."

I could tell I'd disappointed the man.

"AVENTURE is a nice boat." Then his face brightened. "She has a very old engine. A Gardner diesel. Classic engine. Air start. You have to pump the air tank by hand for a half hour before you can start the engine. But it usually starts on the first try.

"Or the second."

I stood up. Sandra stood up. We looked at the door.

"I don't know if I have time today to see AVENTURE," Jean Claude said, looking at his watch. "I think she's in Carcassone, or at least somewhere on the Canal du Midi."

I wasn't quite sure where Carcassone was. The Canal du Midi was in the south. The way south. Like the Mediterranean. Somewhere that most certainly was not Bourgogne.

I sat down. Sandra sat down.

Sandra was close to her limit.

"Is there any barge here, right here, we could walk to and see?" she pleaded. "Today."

Jean Claude looked at her as if she were a mad woman. "Certaine-ment," he mumbled, disappointed. "There are many boats moored here."

He stood up. We stood up.

"I don't think any of them are for sale. But you never know. Maybe somebody will want to sell his boat," he said.

As we walked from his office, with the slight possibility that we might see our first barge, I glanced back at the desk and the telephone where the red "hold" light was still flashing. I wondered whether Jean Claude's best client had extinguished the fire in his engine room.

EDITORIAL NOTE: Confession time. Some names in this book are changed, as Jack Webb warned viewers of Dragnet in 1955, to protect the innocent. More are changed to protect the guilty. OK. Confession. Names are changed to keep folks I might vaguely allude to from striking us from their social lists. We're part of a small, close, gossipy bargee community, what we refer to as "a linear village," on the canals. Be as-sured, nonetheless, that I'm real. So is Sandra. Everybody else I mention is a complete, total figment of my imagination with no relationship to any person or entity living or dead and any such reference is purely coincidental and of no legal consequence. Can you tell I used to be a lawyer. So I'll repeat. Nobody - well maybe not quite nobody - is real in this book. Especially you, that nasty women at the train station in Nuits-St.-George who on a miserably cold, rainy November day refused to unlock the station door and made us wait for the train hunched over in the deluge.

Plan B

We chose Plan B for retirement - live on a canal barge in France - because we each had our own, diametrically, and geographically, opposed Plans A. I wanted to sail around the world. On our sailboat. Like Magellan. But without dying halfway around, of course. We got as far from home in Massachusetts as the Abaco Islands in the Bahamas when Sandra inserted a clause into my Plan A. OK, she said, we can sail around the world. But only if we're never out of sight of land. Sailing through typhoons for week after week is your thing, not mine.

Sandra's Alternate Plan A featured a flat in London, perhaps in Notting Hill. Where Mary Poppins likely retired. London. On shore. In a cozy apartment. With a fireplace. Scones for breakfast.

So we wrote a list of our compromises, the precursor of dozens of subsequent lists. A boat. In Europe. Reasonably comfortable. Within spitting distance of land. Interesting. Exciting. Challenging.

Not death defying.

The solution: nineteen months and then two more summers traveling through French canals and rivers on Hoop Doet Leven ("Hope Gives

Life" in Dutch, "I Hope It Floats" in my mind), a 21 meter (70 foot) steel canal barge built in the Netherlands in 1926.

That rusty old boat and our immersion in French rural living transformed two typically stressed out American baby boomers, dipping their toes in the unknown waters of retirement. There are lessons here, lessons from centuries of French country customs, lessons about making the effort to create a new life in retirement that is as - or more - fulfilling than working life had been, and, most importantly, lessons about a couple who had led interesting but divergent lives learning to live within a few feet of each other and meet shared challenges in a new country with a new language neither of us spoke.

Compromise wasn't all that bad. Certainly, the food was better than starvation rations at sea. And the wine. And the people. And the countryside. And did I mention the wine?

Barging into France

Retirement, as with less pleasant events in life. happens. Sometimes calmly, inevitably, set the new gold watch to daylight savings time, pack your desk into a cardboard box and turn in the magnetic card that opens the office door on weekends. Sometimes, however, the transition is dramatic, like leaping from the sauna into a snow bank.

One Monday morning in February I stood before the United States Supreme Court and told Justice Antonin Scalia that, with all due respect (which is legalese for what a moron I think you are, your honor) I disagree with you on that constitutional issue. It was a bread and butter case for a civil rights lawyer: challenging mandatory male-only registration of eighteen-year-olds with the Selective Service System. That was Monday. First thing Tuesday morning every suit and tie I owned was in trash bags on our front porch, waiting to be picked up by the Big Brothers and Big Sisters charity. The next weekend we were at Charles DeGaulle Airport in Paris, stuffing the rental Renault with two years' of clothing, tools, books and barge equipment to drive to Hoop Doet Leven at the marina in Toul, in Lorraine.

We retired. Like leaping from the sauna to the snow bank.

The drive to the barge took five hours. The planning took two years.

14

In my elementary school days there was a Children's Classic Illustrated Book, part of my mother's rather rudimentary regime for injecting culture - which was pronounced in her Brooklyn accent as "cultcha" - into her offspring, a book called Hans Brinker or the Silver Skates in which Dutch kids spent their winters racing on ice skates along canals. I must have read that book six times. It had not a word about boats on the canals. Nonetheless, Hans Brinker planted the notion of European canals into my boating consciousness, a notion that lay dormant for forty-five or so years until it emerged as the Plan B solution to our two Plans A dilemma.

It turns out there are 8,000 kilometers (5,000 or so miles) of navigable waterways in France alone. And more in England and Germany and Belgium and Holland and, for all we knew, Russia and Moldavia.

Fairly effortlessly we came up with the concept that the way to (1) retire on a boat, and (2) always keep the boat within sight, if not spitting distance, of land, and (3) get Sandra to Europe, if not London, was to surround the boat, and surround Sandra, with France.

Voila. Which, as we came to learn, the French say every fifteen minutes.

So began our barge research. The first concept, a pleasant one, was that what is called a barge in the United States - a fairly unboatlike floating warehouse that gets pushed, pulled and maneuvered by tugboats - is a far cry from what the Europeans call a barge. The U.S. version, when it is seen in Europe, is referred to as a "dumb barge." Not dumb as in deaf and dumb. Dumb as in stupid. As in barely a boat. As in something that floats but can't move on its own without the help of a real boat.

Americans though we were, we would have nothing to do with a dumb barge. Barges in Europe were far from dumb. Even the Queen of England has a barge, called, for obvious reasons, the Royal Barge. Spiffy. Lots of gold. Not at all dumb.

No, we quickly learned, what we wanted was a canal boat. The French call it a peniche (pronounced pen-eesh). So, put aside any notions of a barge as the floating trash trucks used to haul New York City garbage. Picture something long - to carry lots of cargo - and narrow - to fit in skinny canal locks - with its own engine - which early on in the Twentieth Century replaced the previous means of propulsion, which were either (a) horses or (b) the barge wife (truly, we've seen photos of wives wearing leather harnesses hauling boats along the canals while the hus-

15

band stood at the wheel. Steering. Smoking. Captaining. Barge wives were great advocates of installing engines).

We learned about barges and barging in France by following the yellow brick road of Google. This quickly led us to barge brokers' web sites, barge owners' web sites and the web site of the DBA, a British organization formerly known as the Dutch Barge Association, an organization that reverted to its initials because it was neither Dutch nor limited to barges. Nonetheless, the DBA and its web site at www.barges.org is the mother lode of information about barges and barging in Europe.

We spent hours surfing from barge site to barge site, emailing links back and forth when we discovered a barge couple's blog of adventures afloat or brokers' listings of former coal barges converted to floating retirement homes.

Excel spreadsheets cross linking interesting boats for sale were created. Prices were tracked. Budgets were scrawled and modified.

Months passed. The concept of living on a canal boat in France for "a long time" bloomed from a wouldn't-that-be-a-neat-idea to an actual plan. Then into a commitment. We would do it, we decided. And not half way, namby pamby extended vacation style. No, no - as the French put it, repeatedly, over and over, and over, no. If we were going to do this, we were going to DO it.

We'd rent out our house for two years so we couldn't return. Buy the boat, don't rent one. Cancel our cell phones at home and lose the numbers we'd had for as long as there had been cell phone numbers. No toe-in-the-water tentative testing for us. No, no, no. Grab the ankles and leap in, cannonball style.

Only one problem.

Neither of us had ever actually seen a barge. We had to address that omission.

So we went to see Jean Claude.

Dipping our toes in French waters

We left Jean Claude around 6:00 p.m.. We'd knocked on the hulls of a few moored barges and were invited on board for our first conversations, and drinks, with in-the-flesh real life barge people. One couple had just arrived from Australia a few weeks earlier and were settling down on their newly-purchased barge. They were one year ahead of us on the same path. We were still innocent and naive. They'd had a few weeks, cold, wet weeks, for the innocence to begin to go stale. They were in the process of scaling down their plans for immediate total remodeling of their boat to focus on more pressing goals. Like where to find a supply of firewood for their heating stove so they could take their three layers of sweaters off. At least when they were tucked under the covers at night.

We didn't raise the question of whether their boat was for sale. They might have been in the recovery stage from boat lust, but the after effects were still lingering.

We also met a retired London cab driver halfway through a complete renovation of his boat's interior. The process had been going on for several years. Unlike the Australian boat, he told us he'd certainly consider the right offer for his boat. We suspected, though, that as with most any house in coastal Maine, where we sailed summers, the For Sale sign was a more or less permanent part of the landscaping on the off chance some stranger with a case of house lust - the landlocked version of boat lust - and a recent inheritance had an overwhelming urge for a wonderful fixer-upper rural retreat. As beautiful as the first half of this barge's restoration looked, we had no interest in undertaking the second half.

As it turned out we would run into both barges - figuratively - and their owners from time to time throughout our future canal meanderings. The community of people living on boats and bouncing around throughout inland France is fairly small, in the low hundreds, and while our nautical Brownian motions appear random, we inevitably interact with each other.

This, our first trip to France to investigate barging, was only partly intended as a shopping expedition. We had more serious business to complete. At the top of our list was acquiring the necessary licenses to operate a barge on the French canals. The whole business of licensing is complicated, so complicated that nobody seems to understand it. At first, we were told that if you have a license from your home country, that license will be honored throughout the European Union.

But not by Germany, which has its own license requirements. (Obtaining even a fishing license in Germany was not dissimilar from passing the bar exam in Massachusetts and, even if successful, the license is limited to one specific lake, pond or river. And one kind of fish. For specific months.)

France, of course, supports all European Union regulatory requirements, as long as they don't apply to France. France administers its own boat license examination, in French only, the difficulty of which depends on the size of the boat you will operate. Except if you are operating a rental boat. Then, since you are in France on vacation with the sole purpose of spending money in France, and since you probably have no boat experience, no license is required. But whoever rents the boat to you must instruct you on everything required to operate a boat in France. But not for more than twenty minutes of instruction.

We tend to keep a good distance from rental boats. And to not share locks with them.

The Netherlands, Germany and Belgium, have their own national licensing schemes. As does Britain. Somehow, all of these individual systems are supposed to blend into a single European Union licensing standard. When we dipped our toes into these waters, that blending was more of a recipe than a completed soufflé.

All of this is in contrast to the U.S. licensing system, which is pretty much no system at all. In most states, adults don't need a license to operate a boat, from a jet ski to a fishing trawler, as long as they aren't carrying passengers for hire. Even if you carry paid passengers, licenses are issued after you pass a written test. Nobody actually observes you on an actual boat. On the water. This is equivalent to giving a drivers license to everybody who passes the written test. With no road exam.

I am licensed - by the U.S. Coast Guard - to take an unlimited number of paying passengers on a boat up to 50 tons up to 200 miles offshore. All based on passing some written exams proving I know, for example, how many fire axes the Coast Guard requires on a boat. The Coast Guard is big on fire axes, with the mandatory number based on your vessel's tonnage.

In a patriotic gesture, we carry a fire ax on our barge in France, although how one extinguishes a fire with an ax was not included on the Coast Guard examination I took. We bought the ax in a Bricomarché, the French version of Home Depot. The label calls it a tomahawk.

In contrast to the land of the free and the home of the brave, the French are not nearly so, shall we say, laissez faire about boat operators' licenses. Some things just are not done, such as violating the Code Civile de Gustation by, for example, removing the meat from a bulot, a spiral sea snail, in a clockwise direction, against the axis of rotation. Similarly, there can be no more serious French faux pas than declining to regulate an aspect of life that begs to be delimited, controlled, sanctioned, systematized, organized, harmonized and made the subject of rules and a source of civil employment.

French is the source of so many beautiful words: haute cuisine, culture, renaissance, mayonnaise, menage au trois. And some more jarring words. (In contrast to the Second President Bush's comment that the socialist French don't even have a word for entrepreneur.) The word "bureaucracy" is nothing to be especially proud of. We came to learn, however, that in order to enjoy the life the French so enjoy in a society having a regulation for absolutely every aspect of life - including driving a barge down its canals - there has to be an exception to every regulation. The key to getting by in this Dr Jekyl and Mr. Hyde system is finding the escape clause to every rule.

The escape clause to obtaining our barge licenses surfaced when we found an English couple who lived on their Dutch barge in northern France. They were doubly licensed as examiners for French nautical licenses and by the Royal Yachting Association as British license examiners. And their barge qualified in both countries as a vessel on which the on-the-water testing could take place. Two days on their barge and we were the proud holders of International Certificates of Competence with Inland Waters CEVNI ("Code Européen des Voies de Navigation Intérieure") certifications issued by the Royal Yachting Association and honored, we were told, by France.

Capitaine Harvey meet Capitaine Sandra. (Women captains present a problem in France having nothing to do with their boat handling skills. "Capitaine," even though it ends with "-ne," typically a feminine ending, is a masculine noun. The guy in charge of a boat is referred to as "le capitaine." Put a woman in charge of a boat and she becomes grammatically incorrect — a significant form of incorrectness in France — because she would have to be referred to as "la capitaine," with the female "la" preceding a masculine word. A serious no, no, no. To my knowledge, this problem has yet to be resolved. The same problem arose when the French began electing women as town mayors, the "maire," a masculine noun for a person always addressed as "monsieur le maire." One town's solution was to refer to its woman mayor as "Madame Monsieur Le Maire.")

Grammatically correct or incorrect, we were both legal at the helm of a canal barge. In France. Not Germany. Or, as will be explained later, on any river that happens to constitute the border between France and Germany.

The last week of our first French expedition was spent on board an actual barge. We'd come across a web site for the barge NILAYA (boat names, for some reason known only to the Phoenicians, who probably used cuneiform capitals for their vessels, are properly written in ALL CAPITALS). NILAYA was owned by Kevin Hartwell, a Brit who'd renovated the former Dutch commercial barge himself. Kevin built two guest cabins on the boat. He takes up to four people at a time on one-week cruises throughout the French canals. We figured a week's cruise with Kevin would give us an introduction to canal life.

Kevin successfully baited the hook, lured us in and, within a few months of our week on NILAYA, he'd found the boat of our dreams for us. Be extremely careful about spending time with Kevin. You could get hooked, too.

We flew home from France, barged, licensed, well fed and ready to take the next step. Buying the barge that would be our home for the next two years.

Finding Hope

The owners of authentic precious items, such as Rolex watches and exuberant natural décolletage, tend to look down their noses at people who purchase cut-rate replicas of the real thing. The same applies, to a greater or lesser extent, to Dutch barges. We were faced with a number of choices in looking for a barge to buy.

The "real thing" in a Dutch barge is an old commercial barge built in the Netherlands. We all know the story of the Dutch boy who spent a night with his finger in the hole in the dike, thereby saving the Netherlands from the North Sea, a story, as it turns out, first publicly revealed in my childhood friend, Hans Brinker or the Silver Skates. Well, as we know from that story, Holland is a low, flat country, protected from the sea by dikes and laced with canals. For centuries, these canals have been the major means of cargo transportation.

Unlike in France where the sizes of canals and barges were standardized by strict regulations - heaven forbid an opportunity to regulate should be left unregulated - in the Netherlands some canals are wider than others, some are deeper than others, some canal bridges are lower than others. This resulted in a potpourri of barges, each suited to the width, depth and bridge height of its local canals. For example, the Luxemotor, with a pointy bow, was one variety. There is even one species of Dutch barge, a Katwijker, with the steering wheel attached horizontally, rather than vertically, so the boat will fit under one exceptionally low local bridge. The tjalk, shaped like a wooden shoe, was another. Here is one barge broker's listing of different types of barges he offers:

Aak, Beurvaartschip, Boieraak, Bolpraam, Boltjalk, Botter, Freycinet, Friee
Tjalk, Groninger,Boltjalk, GroningerTjalk, Hagenaar,Haseteraak, Humber , Ijsselaak, Ijsseltjalk, Kempenaar, Klipper, KlipperAak, Kotter, Kraak, Le msteraak, Luxemotor, Midi, Paviljoentjalk, Peniche, RiverBarge, Schoener , Skutsje, Spits, Steilsteven, Thames, Tjalk, Westlander, and Zeetjalk.

Who knew? All we thought we wanted was a "barge."

In the 1950s the Dutch government finally got around to scrutinizing this nautical mishmash. It was decided by the powers that be (or had been) that fewer larger barges would be more efficient than many smaller barges of idiosyncratic shapes and sizes. The government offered financial incentives to barge owners to take their small boats out of service and replace them with large, uniform commercial vessels.

This resulted in a flood of out-of-service smaller Dutch barges. Some sank. Some were cut up for scrap metal. Some were turned into fixed floating homes, restaurants or bars.

Some became live-aboard canal boats. These old Dutch barges, mostly built before 1930 as commercial vessels for the transportation of goods, from coal to tulip bulbs, are the kind of "Dutch barge" we were looking for.

The quality of the transmogrification from coal barge to luxury cruising boat varies from boat to boat. Some are fairly, shall we say, crude. As in having "tube toilets," literally a tube from the toilet bowl rim down to the water. Some are high end, floating penthouses.

Because these barges were designed to operate entirely on canals, squeezing under low bridges and through skinny locks, and to be operated by a husband and wife crew, they are perfectly suited for our intended cruising. They fit the locks like corks in a wine bottle. Their flat, straight sides let them lie calmly against the sides of locks, unlike sleek sailboats or motor yachts with racy hydrodynamic curves. Their flat bottoms, while uncomfortable in rough water, are perfect for quiet, shallow canals. Their heavy, slow turning engines with large propellers match the slow speeds of canals. All the bits and pieces for handling the boats in canal locks are in the proper places.

Because Dutch barges are so well designed for cruising canals and because some people prefer their antiques on their mantels rather than as their floating homes, an industry has developed in building "replica" Dutch barges. These look more or less like the real thing but they have modern engines, wiring and fittings. They are insulated with modern material, rather than 90-year-old Amsterdam newspapers stuffed behind the walls, and their kitchens and bathrooms look like modern kitchens and bathrooms.

A replica barge was an option for us to consider.

Briefly.

Remember, we decided to do this whole barge thing whole hog. Straight from the sauna into the snow bank. And we were coming from old wood boats. No, no, no. For us it would be an old iron boat. With a history. With character. With rust. With wires that entered a hole in the wall in one color and magically came out the other side a totally different color. With an old diesel engine that makes a sound that translated from Dutch sounds remarkably like "I think I can, I think I can."

Those are the boats we looked at on line. And those are the boats we hunted down, like rare wild creatures on the veldt, on shopping trips to France. We almost settled on a boat once, but backed out, knowing that "our" boat was out there, lurking somewhere in France. If we didn't find our boat, it would find us. This was to be a mystical adventure. We were confident.

Voila. (Add "voila" to your vocabulary and you'll automatically be a happier person. It feels so nice to say.)

Kevin Hartwell, on NILAYA, had been keeping a barge-like eye peeled on our behalf as he cruised his guests throughout France. One day I received an email from Kevin with the caption of "I found your boat." Attached were fifty photos Kevin had taken of HOOP DOET LEVEN, which was moored right behind NILAYA at Verdun, the site of the ferocious World War One battle. Kevin said HOOP was owned by two Americans from Texas who'd mentioned to him, over drinks, that they were thinking of testing the market at the end of the summer. Kevin said he knew two Americans who would buy their boat.

Two weeks later we flew to France for a rendezvous with HOOP. We made an appointment to meet Bud and Joyce, who'd owned HOOP for eleven years, at Epernay in Champagne. The appointment was on our kitchen calendar. In red magic marker. Highlighted in yellow. Balloons. Arrows. You know the drill. Saturday morning in Epernay. HOOP. At 9:00 a.m.

Boat lust. Its a beautiful thing. We checked into our hotel in Epernay the night before and couldn't restrain ourselves. A night-time reconnaissance mission was in order. We spotted HOOP from a distance. Crossed to the far side of the canal from where it was moored. Lurked behind some bushes and peered through the branches. Didn't want Bud and Joyce to figure we were too hot to trot. Zoomed the camera to full telephoto and shot twenty photos.

Kneeling in the mud, scratched by the branches that hid us from citizens who might wonder about a couple of Americans lurking in the canal side shrubs as darkness fell, Sandra and I came to a simultaneous conclusion. We'd found our barge.

Boat lust.

The rest was anticlimactic. We spent most of the next day on the boat, dutifully looking through cabins and closets. Crawling around the engine room. Checking all the appliances and fixtures. Going through the motions. But we both knew. We knew before we'd crawled out from the shrubbery. All that was left, besides such perfunctory matters as agreeing to a price, signing a contract and having a professional surveyor confirm that the boat would continue to float, was one final step.

We had to pass the interview.

Bud and Joyce were not about to sell HOOP DOET LEVEN to whoever traipsed over the transom, cash in hand. No, we had to go through more than a job interview, more than a college admission interview. Maybe slightly less intense than the inquisition one puts one's daughter's betrothed through. But only slightly less intense.

They took us to dinner and questioned us for hours. In twenty-five words or less why do you love France. Tell us about every boat you've owned. Answer this: the engine runs rough, black smoke comes from the stack and the hot water in the kitchen sink doesn't get hot. What is wrong? Maybe not quite those exact questions.

And they told us stories about their eleven years in France, returning to Texas for the winters (HOOP has a top flight barbecue on the stern deck, a benefit of buying from Texans.) We were hooked. We were ready.

And we were approved.

They cruised on HOOP the remainder of the summer, winding up at a boat yard in Toul, near Nancy, where the boat was tied up for the winter. They took eleven years of memories when they left.

HOOP was waiting for us. We were waiting for France. It was a long winter.

Life in three piles

It took the highest court in the nation to keep us from leaving for France.

The original plan was to celebrate the new year in France, on board HOOP. My legal practice was almost entirely wound down. I resolved the outstanding cases I could resolve. Transferred the unresolved cases to other lawyers. It was down to one final case at the end of a career in civil rights litigation, rattling cages and making the world a better place for all people, regardless of the planet of their birth. The last case was pretty much where I'd started in civil rights, back in the Sixties when, along with many of my generation, I burned my draft card and challenged the Selective Service System during the Vietnam War.

Now I was challenging the last vestiges of the military draft, a law that required 18-year-old men to register in case a draft were reinstated. Women, despite making up 18 percent of America's military, were forbidden from registering with Selective Service. As a relic of Cold War days, a law banned those men who had never registered from ever working for the government.

I represented a group of federal employees, some of whom had worked for the government for more than twenty years, who were fired when it was discovered they had never registered with Selective Service when they were 18. It is always a tough task convincing a court to declare a law unconstitutional. This was an especially tough one.

I'd won in the lower federal court, where a judge declared the law violated an obscure provision of the U.S. Constitution that prohibited Congress from enacting bills of attainder. This is so obscure that without getting into just what constitutes a bill of attainder, I'll admit that most of my legal research involved scouring a database of British Acts of Parliament from before the Battle of Bunker Hill.

The government appealed and the appeals court reversed the trial judge, on what I thought was a rather picayune technical jurisdiction issue. That was the end of the case. We were free to flee the country and fly to France.

Until three women and six men in black robes - the United States Supreme Court - selected this case (admittedly at my request) to be one of the 73 cases they'd hear that year, out of about 9,000 applications. Be careful what you ask for. You might get it. The argument was scheduled for the end of February. Appearing before the Supreme Court is a big deal for a lawyer. I'd done it once before. This would be my last appearance before any court. Ever. Talk about going out with a bang.

Bang.

I was out.

The next week was a frenzy of preparing to leave the country for two years. Our lives were sorted into three piles:

• Pile Number One – This was going to France with us. Besides clothing, we packed everything from a 3G wireless router with the "Hoop" network already set up, to France-compatible Apple adapters for our all-Apple electronic lives, to Sandra's favorite essential kitchen tools, including her rotating chicken timer and her favorite can opener, which, it turned out one evening as she was preparing her first dinner onboard for French guests, would not open French cans. The clothing decisions took into consideration that we'd spend two winters in France.

• Pile Number Two: This got stored away in Ipswich, either in our new storage room in the basement or in an upstairs loft.

• Pile Number Three: This was all the detritus of twenty years of living in the same house, things that hadn't surfaced in years but had been stored away just in case. Now it was all either recycled, taken to the town dump or donated to Big Brother, Big Sister. Included in the donation bags were just about all of my lawyer suits, the kind I wore, not the kind I filed in court.

It is a cathartic experience to sort all your possessions this way. And it shows how much we accumulate that we certainly never needed (except for all the priceless parts that came off a fleet of old wooden boats, including every rusty washer and bolt, just in case. That was all stored in the basement. Just in case.)

A week after standing before the Supreme Court, we were climbing onto our new home, HOOP DOET LEVEN. Our first night on board was everything we'd hoped and dreamed for. France. On our own boat. With fresh baguettes, creamy cheeses, cafes, accordions. Everything.

Except heat.

No coupling

Early March in Northern France is not quite arctic. But neither is it tropical. One thing became clear right away. Whoever wrote that lovely song lyric about "I love Paris in the Springtime" had never been to Paris, or France in the Springtime. March is cold. And rainy. And gray. Exceedingly, depressingly gray. A climate that calls out for huddling around the heating stove.

Gray French winters explain why the French invention of existentialism was inevitable.

HOOP has a fantastic French Godin heating stove in the main cabin, a creature of iron and brass connected to a 500 liter diesel tank that drips fuel a drop at a time into a chamber where it burns with a subtle blue flame that drives the chilblains from the barge and the frost from the windows.

When it works.

When we arrived at the boat the Godin didn't work.

And thus we received our first lesson in the joys and surprises of living on an 86-year-old boat, a vessel on which generations of clever, handy men and women had utilized their cleverness and handiness to resolve decades of seemingly insurmountable glitches, what the French call "un pépin technique."

Like getting the diesel fuel from the big tank in the engine room to the beautiful stove in the main salon. It turned out there was a small electric pump mounted to a steel frame in the engine room next to the fuel tank. A copper pipe ran out of the fuel tank to the pump, and then from the pump down into the boat's bilge, to emerge through the floor next to the Godin heating stove.

The problem was that instead of the stove getting hot when the fuel pump switch was turned on, the pump got hot. Red hot. Then it smoked. And died.

Perhaps on a production boat, built on an assembly line in some boat factory, or even on a "replica" barge, built three months ago in a modern boat yard, that fuel pump would be listed on the parts inventory as a standard issue marine fuel pump for diesel heating stoves. You would probably have a choice of colors from the pump catalog.

Our pump, however, was likely added to HOOP's inventory sometime when I was in college, or my father was. It most certainly did not come from a boat supply catalog. It did have some obscure numbers on it but any bits and pieces of anything resembling a label had long since evaporated, probably around the time of the Korean War.

Fortunately, we had a good internet connection at Lorraine Marine, where HOOP spent the winter. A few hours of paleontological research revealed that the closest facsimile of the dead pump was a fuel pump on an early 1960s MG sports car. I could accept that. I'd once owned a sailboat that survived several trouble free years with an electrical distributor on its engine that had come out of a Maine mechanic's pick-up truck when the original one on the boat's engine gave up the ghost.

Locating an early 1960s MG fuel pump was none too difficult in neighboring England and within a few days a shiny new pump arrived by express. And it looked like if not the identical twin of the dead pump, at least a kissing cousin. Out with the old (or olde) and in with the new. And a new problem.

The tube coming from the diesel tank to the pump was fitted with a French, metric fitting. The MG pump had an older British not-metric fitting. They were just different enough that an equal amount of diesel pumped out of the connection as through it.

A visit to a hardware store was in order.

Sandra's French was pretty good at that point. Not nearly as good as it was to become, but comprehensible. For things simple. She'd spent two months the past winter at a French immersion program in Villefranche-sur-Mer, on the French Riviera. Intensive immersion. Students were fined one euro for every word they spoke in a language other than French.

We both went to the hardware store. Sandra explained our problem and we were handed a threaded tube that failed to fit anything on the barge.

I then went to the town's plumbing supply store to plead my case, primed by Sandra with a collection of French phrases. My French at that point was primarily based on viewing hours of videotapes of Marcel Marceau, the French mime. I basically spoke in English with an accent that was a cross between Pepi Le Pew and Inspector Clouceau. Hercule Poirot when all else failed. And lots of smiles and apologies.

When my turn at the counter arrived I explained, or thought I explained, that the fitting I held in my right hand was Francais. The fitting in my left hand was Anglais. Je voudrais - I would like - a coupler, which Sandra had looked up to be, voila, a coupleur ("coop-lur" as Inspector Clouceau would say).

The two men behind the counter consulted in rapid French, much too fast for me to hope to follow. Much hand movement and head shaking was involved. They retrieved the two parts from me and brought them to a third man. After heated discussion, one man was delegated to deal with me.

Vous êtes Anglais, I was asked, a stern expression on his face. Are you English?

No, I replied. American.

He broke into a grin and reported this additional, seemingly highly relevant information to his compatriots. More conversation followed.

Finally, the original delegate returned. Je suis desolé, he said. I am sorry. Anglais et Francais ne pas couple. The English and the French do not couple. Never. Absolutely never. This fact of life was explained to me as if I should have been aware of hundreds of years of one nation or the other conquering one nation or the other. There was to be no coupling between the French and the English.

I persevered and eventually the three men returned with several handfuls of bronze fittings and threaded items that, put together in the correct order, should solve my problem, hopefully with generous lubricant and protection between the two nations at the point of actual coupling.

And it worked.

Let there be heat.

Like the
Statue of Liberty

With a week on board HOOP under our belts we were feeling comfortable. Heat, light, water, bread, wine and new friends. We had to be under way by the beginning of April as the canal authority, the VNF, the Voies Navigables de France, announced that the section of the Canal de la Marne au Rhin on which HOOP was moored was to be drained. Yes, all the water would be let out. For maintenance. We had to vacate that section of the canal by April 1 or we'd spend a month sitting in the mud. Nothing subtle about that.

Before we left, however, we had a mission. My cardiologist in Boston had arranged an appointment for me with a French cardiologist in nearby Nancy so I could obtain French prescriptions for a few medications. We still had our rental car and Nancy was a half hour drive from Toul.

Just as we got on the highway between the two cities we felt the rental car stutter, mutter, complain and just say no. It turned out that when we'd requested a diesel car (it was an Audi A1, the smaller sister of what we know as an A4) and when we'd confirmed that the car took gazole (French for diesel) and that the tag attached to the keys said diesel, well, the woman at Europecar at Charles de Gaulle Airport was just being polite when she'd said that of course that was so. The car was not a diesel at all and it didn't enjoy being fed diesel fuel. The car died on a highway bridge just outside Toul. Fortunately, a short walk away was a gendarmerie, a station of the national police force. We walked there and told our story. Even though it was that most sacred of French times – lunch – three officers helped and suffered through long phone calls with Europecar, laughing about the on-hold music. Eventually, an arrangement was negotiated in which a taxi came to take me to my doctor's appointment and to drop Sandra off on the highway at the car to wait for a tow truck.

That led to separate misadventures. Sandra rode with the tow truck driver – whose only English words were "New York" – to his garage where he pumped out the diesel, poured some gasoline into the tank and got the engine started, a process that took a few hours because he had to tell about his wife, his children, the state of French politics and then spend a half hour or so figuring out what to charge. Mostly, he wanted to know about New York, where Sandra lived in younger and wilder days. Eventually, the car started, now with gasoline, Sandra drove to a gas station and filled up, then drove to Nancy to rendezvous with me.

I, meanwhile, was in a taxi with a woman driver who the less she understood me the faster she spoke, which simply meant I failed to understand more words. Our miscommunication included such basic items as which city my doctor was in. Eventually we arrived at the medical center for the cardiology appointment, my first encounter with French medicine. Having in mind that my last medical encounter was at Brigham & Womens Hospital in Boston, a Harvard Medical School teaching hospital, about as fine as medicine gets, L'Institut Lorraine du Cœur et des Vaisseaux was on the same scale. And my French doctor turned out to be not only the director of the entire Institute, but one of Europe's leading cardiologists. Overkill just for getting new prescriptions but a truly nice person. He spoke English but it did not seem any of the staff did. With Sandra – my constant translator – last seen lonely and forlorn through the rear window of the taxi abandoned on a highway bridge waiting for the tow truck, I was left to communicate with my Marcel Marceau French. First came the visit to the intake office, where the three women made it clear that payment would be required for a person not covered by the French medical system, then they wanted to know all about my boat – which uncomfortably was pronounced as "your bitch" – and they made it clear they were excited about having an American patient, even though the computer system would not accept my address because my postal ZIP code in Massachusetts, strangely enough, did not match any French postal code.

I was ushered to the doctor, nonetheless.

Afterwards came the matter of payment. Forms were filled out, consultations were performed, and, at last, five people from various offices and departments gathered to confer, all while I stood, credit card in hand. Forty minutes later a decision was announced: it will all – EKG, physical examination, consultation, prescriptions – be a "cadeau de France." "Cadeau, I don't know that word," I replied in pidgin-French. The response, "Eet iz like ze Statute of Liberty, a present from France," I was told, "It is gratuit." No charge. A quick "vive la France" and I was off to Nancy to meet Sandra and the now-gasoline-powered Audi.

The struggles in the United States with instituting Obamacare, a baby step toward a rational national health care system, contrasted with every one of our encounters with French health care. Prices for doctors, hospitals, lab tests and medications were, to us, laughingly low. Pharmacists apologized to us when we told them our medication costs would not be reimbursed. Some offered to cut their prices. We declined and explained that the full cost of medications in France was less than the patient co-pay under our through-the-roof expensive medical insurance in Massachusetts. Remember, Romneycare came before Obamacare.

Prescriptions in hand, we were ready to set off on the canals, at long last.

Under way at last

We spent three weeks moored fifty feet from a canal lock in Toul. A canal lock that looked just about exactly as wide as our barge. A canal lock with stone walls that looked hard as, well, hard as stone. This presence loomed over us for those three weeks. I was intimidated. I was used to the wide open seas. I was comfortable when the only thing in sight was water.

I would walk over to the lock and stare it down. Picture just how we'd drive the barge in. Just where we'd tie each mooring line.

Our day of departure approached. The plan was to head for the Dutch Barge Association - the DBA - summer rally in Paris. We had six weeks to get there, six weeks in April and May when canal traffic would be light and we

could make our mistakes with few witnesses.

But first we had to get through Lock Number One.

And after this lock, our first day required us to climb from the Moselle River valley, where Toul was, up to a ridge that marked the start of the Meuse River valley. This involved twenty canal locks and, for good measure, an 800 meter tunnel.

Working a barge through a canal lock - a French lock is called an ecluse, the lock tender is, of course, le eclusier - was a major part of our two-day hands on licensing course, and we'd done a week of locks on NILAYA. But we'd never done a lock by ourselves. To make matters a tad more complicated, these locks had been automated. We were handed a device that looked like a garage door opener and told to aim it at the lock just before we reached it. The lock would open automatically, we'd been told.

Right. We believed that. What it really meant was that there would be nobody, no eclusier, around to help us when the inevitable disaster happened. We were on our own.

We hadn't counted on the subtle kindliness of French people in the countryside.

Passing through the dreaded First Lock we met two workmen dressed in VNF blue and green coveralls, who stood at the lock watching us. As with all encounters French, speaking with them involved numerous bonjours, bon journée s, monsieurs and madames and au revoirs, interlaced with rapid and indecipherable friendly French. Then I, in my best Hercule Poirot French accent, said this was "ma première ecluse," my first lock in my new bateau. Word passed rapidly on the VNF grapevine and by our third lock we'd acquired a friendly VNF guy in his VNF van who just happened to be driving from lock to lock all day at the same slow pace we were traveling. He just happened to appear at each lock when Sandra missed lassoing a bollard, just in time to place her loop where she intended. When I couldn't reach the lever to start the lock cycling, voila, it cycled anyway. By our twentieth lock of the day, our guardian angel was still appearing to shepherd us through.

By afternoon, we'd passed through all twenty locks with a few bumps and scrapes to our 86-year-old barge, but with no visible scars. Then at the top of the flight of locks we faced an 800 meter tunnel through the hill separating the two valleys. We emerged onto the Meuse

River, heading north toward historic World War One battlefields, Verdun, Sedan, the Ardennes, spending the night in the small village of Pagny-sur-Meuse.

This town boasts of La Favorite, a favorite French truck stop. On the theory that truckers know their food, and the realization that the town had no other place to eat, we stopped there, too. The buffet explained why it was so popular with the truckers.

There we were, ready to celebrate our first day actually traveling on the canals, so Sandra, in her best French, asked the waitress for a wine suggestion. The poor frazzled woman, compelled to deal with a couple of Americans while running back and forth from a 20-foot table surrounded by an ever-changing cast of truck drivers, uttered an untranslatable French "poof" sound and pointed to the end of the buffet table. I walked over to examine where she was pointing. I stood in line behind three truckers. Each man held a pitcher in each hand. Picture the local House of Pizza. You order your pizza and are asked whether you're having a drink. You say sure, I'll have a small soda and you are handed a paper cup, which you carry to the device that has a row of nozzles for Coke, Diet Coke, root beer, orange stuff and ginger ale. Ice dispenser in the middle. The wine fountain at La Favorite was exactly the same, except it only had three nozzles: rouge, blanc and rosé. No Glasses. Only pitchers.

The truckers carried their pairs of topped-up pitchers back to the long table, where they whispered nonstop to one another. As one trucker stood and left, he shook hands all around. As another trucker arrived he shook hands all around, kissing some men on both cheeks.

A place not yet on the Rick Steeves tourist radar.

Sandra and I looked at each. I filled her glass from the pitcher of vin blanc. Grinned. We were in France. On our boat. The pinch-me moments had begun.

Catastrophe

Catastrophe (in French with a silent "e") struck the next morning in Pagny-sur-Meuse, a tiny ville with only the barest essentials: a pharmacy, a hairdresser, a dog groomer, a cafe and a boulangerie (bread bakery). We woke to a cloudy, chilly morning. I trudged to the boulangerie for our morning croissants. The town was eerily still. Streets empty. No cars. No people. Plague? War? No, worse. The boulangerie was closed. Closed at 7:30 a.m. Why would any sane person, meaning other than Americans, be on the street if the boulangerie were closed? I beat a retreat to the barge, we had our coffee and tea and, hungry, deprived, started the engine and motored away toward Commercy, a city that would have boulangeries on every corner, as is proper.

The barge, too, was put off by the morning's disaster. As we reached the bottom of our third lock, as the gates in front of us were opening after we'd been lowered five meters as we headed down the Meuse, the engine burped and died. A descent down the ladder into the engine room showed a coolant hose had let lose, spilling, again, all the coolant into the engine oil pan. What to do with a dead engine sitting at the bottom of a lock, 15 feet of stone walls on either side of us? It was noon, what else could be done but lunch. We dined in the wheelhouse tied at the bottom of the lock. After, we fixed the engine and motored down the canal to Commercy.

Commercy is a city with pride. We were in Lorraine now, posters of the eponymous quiche are on walls, people were panting in anticipation of what President Sarkozy declared was the 600th anniversary of the birth of Joan of Arc (pronounced in one breath as "Jondar"), the Maid of Lorraine who saved (almost) France from the English, a declaration inexplicably touted as a campaign nod to conservatives. Commercy, going one step further, was also the home of the madeleine, a yummy spongy cookie named after the mother of King Louis XV's chef. They're everywhere there. The streets are paved with them. They grow on trees. We motored past the official madeleine bakery on the canal and had to increase throttle to push through the powerful aroma. We bought a tub of 500 of them. Well almost 500. And began eating our way through.

Summer would likely be busy here but in April we had the town dock all to ourselves. This is a typical location, a long dock right in the heart of town, with water and electricity, and wifi (pronounced by the French as "wee-fee") for free. Imagine pulling into a city marina in the States on a 70-foot boat and not being charged. We liked it so much we stayed four nights. City on one side, fields on the other, the River Meuse in front of us.

The mooring is located in a park, the key feature of which is a high stone wall that circles around . . . something. We climbed to the road and looked down on what a signed proclaimed as the Commercy Velodrome, a bicycle racing track with high, steeply banked walls. This is French NASCAR, on bicycles and with better food. The sign says the Velodrome was built in 1946. One would think that a village in eastern France, not all that far from the German border, would have had more important things to do in 1946 than to construct a velodrome. Ah, but the sign says it was built by German prisoners of war, which suggests an interesting conversation back then:

Fritz: Zo, Herman, iv de var haz been over for a year, vy are ve shtill in France? I vant to go home to Gretel und der kinder.

Herman: Ze French say ve must rebuild zair country before ve can go back to Germany.

Fritz: Ach de leiber, Herman, zat vill take years. France is in ruins. I vill never zee Gretel.

Herman: Not to vorry, Fritzie. Zay say not to zink about rebuilding the city. Zay vant to race bicycles first. Zen ve go home.

41

French immersion

Before we get much deeper into tales of the French countryside, a word on the French language is in order. A word is about all I can manage. Not always the same word. Actually, not always an actual word. I ordered what to my highly trained ear sounded like a mushroom (champignon) omelet at lunch our first day in Commercy. It came with ham (jambon), no mushrooms. Close enough. Delicious. As was the pitcher of house wine. And the salad. And the cafe gourmand that Sandra ordered (coffee with a dessert potpourri). But, par usual, I digress to food (the most-heard words in our restaurant eavesdropping are "mange" (eat) and "vacance" (vacation). Hadn't heard "Sarkozy" once).

So back to language. Sandra worked at it. She studied at the French Library in Boston. Used her remedial reading teacher skills to teach herself. She goes through her 1,400 favorite French words on her iPhone flashcards. She reads La Monde online every morning. To top it off, she went to a French language immersion school on the Cote d'Azur in November for a month, and stayed for two months. She speaks. They understand, generally. They speak. She pretends to understand. Somehow communication occurs, although in her first effort to buy stamps she told the postmistress she wanted to mail herself to America. Immersion is an interesting concept. The immersion program Sandra went through involved intensive, nothing-but-French instruction eight hours a day. Another form of immersion could be religious, as in born-again full body

42

baptism. My language program followed the more common meaning of immersion, as in "over-your-head," or simply, "drowning."

French is difficult, far more difficult than my six years of Russian in Fair Lawn, New Jersey public schools, the education system's response to Sputnik. Certainly tougher than Swahili 1A had been at Syracuse University, where the instructor had been Miss Kenya in the Miss Universe contest the prior year (there might be a more shallow reason for studying a language, but none comes to mind).

French workers are prohibited from working more than 35 hours a week or 46 weeks a year, understandably, because they need the rest of their time to speak French. There are letters in the French alphabet that have not been heard out loud since Caesar defeated the Gauls. Our rule for pronunciation is "if in doubt, leave it out." The last two letters of a word are rarely pronounced. Often, the first two letters are not pronounced. That means that most three- and four-letter words are simply thought, but never spoken. Not only are most letters not pronounced, but the spaces between words are left out, too. Entire paragraphs are merged into one spoken sound, involving continuous movements of cheeks, lips, eyebrows, ear wiggling, squeezing of the shoulders, rumbling of the esophagus, occasionally, it seems, some sort of finger snapping action.

Even the simplest things are difficult. Here is a list:

1. No, that "1" isn't the first item on the list. It is the first problem, saying "one." One is spelled "un." (Or "une.") "Un" is pronounced several dozen different ways, depending on whether the one of what you want is masculine or feminine, past, present or in England, in which case you don't really want it. Whether you use the masculine or feminine forms of "one" bears no relation to whether the "one" you are referring to is masculine or feminine in reality. "Barbe," meaning beard, is feminine. "Vagin," meaning vagina, is masculine. Don't think about that too deeply. Describing your husband as "le mari," (masculine) means he's your husband. Calling him "la mari" (feminine) means "marijuana."

Getting back to "one." Pronouncing "un" properly involves forming the mental image of four days of constipation leading up to the absolute necessity of finding relief so that you squat down, knees bent, clench your posterior muscles and squeeze as if it is your last chance of escaping unpleasant medical complications until you finally part your lips and let forth with an "unghhhn" sound from the recesses of your throat, vibrating your adams apple slightly and exhaling with your best yogic force.

If you are lucky, that sound will get you one café. Better, I have found, to always buy two of anything.

Incidents of bungled French, almost always met with warm smiles and appreciation, if not comprehension, were virtually a daily happening. Here's an example. At the Bricomarché, which is how you say Home Depot in French, I asked the clerk for flexible plastic tubing to cover electrical wires for the solar panels I was installing on the barge. I described what I wanted as un preservatif pour les cables electrique. She smiled and asked how much I wanted. I replied 5 meters. Oo la la, she said. Turns out I'd told her I wanted a 15 foot condom.

I suspect she repeated that story. I certainly have. And I did receive some strange, pleasantly strange, glances from French women in town. Or maybe that's just my imagination.

But I got better at it. Dogs, scientists say, have evolved to the point where they can sense human communication by the speaker's tone, pace, body language and context, and especially the emotional emphasis of the speech. This placed me on the communication level of a clever poodle. We could usually get the sense of what was being said to us, and each day got better. Of course, that clever poodle would receive the same message from "let's go to the cafe so you can sit on a chair and order snails, ok, Fifi, oo la la" as she'd get from "I'm taking you to the boucherie to be turned into poodle pate'" if both were spoken with the same enthusiasm.

I am in the same boat as Fifi when it came to that problem. Come to think of it, they probably enjoy poodle pate' somewhere in France.

The wild mooring

We continued our journey down the River Meuse. Most nights we stopped in a town. Most towns have a place to tie up, either a formal halte fluvial (a stopping place for boats) or a spontaneous place to tie up, perhaps an abandoned commercial loading dock with bollards or rings to tie to. There is almost never a charge to moor overnight. Often there is free

water to top off our tank. Sometimes there is electricity.

Always there is a boulangerie for our endless baguettes. And always there is a cafe, for a glass of wine or a beer in the afternoon or a tiny cup of espresso, which comes with a cookie or chocolate. Some towns have a restaurant, usually just a husband and wife business, she in the dining room greeting and serving, he in the kitchen, creating. You order only the day's "menu," three courses, including dessert, which may be sweet or may be a plate of cheeses. Wine is extra. The wine list may be long but is likely to be short. You don't order from the wine list. You order a pichet, a small pitcher, of white or red. The owner knows what wine to serve with his food. You let him decide. He is never wrong. Dinner takes at least two hours. There is no way to rush it. Coffee comes only after dessert has been cleared. Americans who want their coffee with dessert must learn to adapt. What they desire is impossible. It cannot and will not happen. You can ask for the check but it will not come for a half hour. If at all. The only way to leave in less than a half hour after coffee is to . . . leave. Get up and walk toward the door. Then the check will come. Otherwise, you wait.

You adapt.

Being in town overnight means a walk to the boulangerie in the chilly morning mist for the day's baguette and morning croissants. The ritual at the boulangerie is as formal as a Japanese tea ceremony. One greets Madame boulangére (it is always a woman, monsieur is out back, baking away). Madame must be greeted formally with "bonjour Madame." Until she is greeted, you fail to exist. She cannot see you. She will not speak to you. On being greeted, she springs to life and responds with a musical bonjour. You comment on the weather. It is cold today, Madame, you say. Madame commiserates, then smiles warmly to reward you for braving the weather to visit her. With greetings exchanged and pleasantries accomplished, you may now ask for your baguette and your croissants, carefully stating whether you want your croissants "natural," which means just butter and flour, or "avec amonde," sprinkled with almond slices, or (my favorite) "au chocolat," a pain au chocolate. She might inquire as to whether you prefer your baguette "bien cuit," well cooked, on the dark side. Oui, s'il vous plaît, you reply because doesn't everybody have a preference as to how well their bread is baked. She searches through the wicker basket in which the long loaves are standing on end until she finds the one baguette done just the way you like it. She either wraps a thin piece of paper around just the center portion or slides it into a paper sleeve that leaves half the loaf exposed. The paper is your handle but you must be able to proudly display your naked baguette as you walk down the street.

A Frenchman's baguette is like an Englishman's umbrella, as decorative as it is essential. Madame hands the baguette to you. She selects your two croissants, places them in a paper bag, pinches her fingers on the two corners of the open end of the bag and twirls the bag around her hands to twist the corners closed. They must teach this maneuver in boulangerie school. She hands you the bag. You respond with merci Madame. She tells you the price. You don't have a clue because French numbers are so difficult (they don't even have a number for 80, but instead say "four twenties." Ninety-five is "four twenties and fifteen.") You place enough money on the counter to cover double what you bought. Never hand Madame money directly. She carefully counts out your change and places it on the counter, even if your hand is held out. You accept your change and say every nice word you know, merci, bonne journée (good day), au revoir. She responds in kind. You both then reply with et vous aussi (the same to you). You glance discreetly at Madame. If she appears satisfied, you may leave. Then the next person in line repeats the entire ritual. Madame smiles warmly when told the weather is cold, as if thanking him for informing her of a fact of which she had been totally unaware.

This is the complete opposite of Dunkin Donuts, where food manufacturing is regimented so the village idiot can produce the same bagel in every store, where the thank you's are mandated by the franchisee operations manual. If you are in a hurry, Dunkin addresses your requirements. The French way is older, slower, more like Alabama, in a good sense, than New York, or Massachusetts.

Each town shares these rituals, yet each town is different.

Some nights, however, we skip the towns. Our first wild mooring, tied to the side of the canal, was several days down the River Meuse, near Verdun, surrounded by pastures and hills, everything green and bursting with the sun evaporating the prior night's spring rain. Cows everywhere, huge white Charolais beef cattle sprinkled like giant marshmallows on the hillsides, black and white Holsteins for milk and, from time to time, Jersey girls, reminiscent of Sandra's buddies from Appleton Farm in our home of Ipswich, where she milked and groomed and was the "cow treat" lady. Knowing she had pockets full of the molasses and oat crunchies she baked for them, the Appleton cows would surround her, nudging their hundred-pound heads against her sides.

We motored that day from Lorraine north into the Ardennes region. The River Meuse had grown wider and deeper, allowing us to rev the engine higher and go a tad faster, from a slow walk to a quick walk, still slower than a six-year-old on his first bike, training wheels and all. As if it were possible, the countryside became even more rural. Towns smaller and farther apart.

We'd yet to encounter another boat.

The river snakes through its valley, twisting and turning in long lazy esses with high hills on both sides, hills covered in pastures sprinkled with cows, cows and more cows. Every herd has at least one member who is fascinated by the barge, watching our slow passage. One herd gallops along, pacing us until stopped by a fence. Others run away from us. Most ignore us.

We tied to the canal bank around noon, after three hours motoring. Nobody was in sight except a farmer on his tractor in the distance. It is quiet here, the only sounds the birds calling, ducks splashing into the water as they land, wind, wind and more wind, making our slow, careful entries into the locks tricky. Sandra stood ready at two locks with our spare tire, a small car tire on a heavy rope, ready to hang from the side as a shock absorber should the wind blow us into the stone walls of the lock.

We walked along the river in the afternoon, seeing a town across the river but no bridge. A hand-lettered sign on the path pointed off toward "Gallo-Roman site" 7.5 kilometers to the side. The sign reminded us that we walked on paths others had walked for eons.

Our home in Ipswich, in Massachusetts, in New England is historic. By American standards. The yellow farm house we see from our kitchen window, across the salt marsh, was built by the foreman of the jury in the Salem witch trials. Sandra discovers 400-year-old Native American arrowheads while digging in her garden.

History here is on a different scale. When hunters were chipping stone tools where Sandra's garden blossoms, in France Moliere was writing Le Misanthrope. People dig in France and find 20,000-year-old Neolithic arrowheads.

Man migrated to America. Humans evolved in France.

We sense this history at the wild mooring. Since the days of Neanderthals and Cro-Magnon men, this river and its valley have been a highway, the only easy path between the hills from south to north. Roman legionnaires marched along this river past where we tied up. Grain was delivered down this river during the Middle Ages, transported in flat barges from the fields of France to cities in Belgium and Holland, farther down the Meuse. German and French armies battled and died in the fields we pass, in 1870, when Germany won, in World Wars I and II, when Germany was defeated. We spot military cemeteries, small and large, on hillsides, miniature versions of Washington's Arlington cemetery. Most are French dead, some say they are American cemeteries, like the one a few days earlier near the Argonne battlefield from World War I. Up what seemed an abandoned dirt road was what a sign said was a German cemetery. So much has happened for thousands of years within sight of where we travel.

And now a couple of Americans float through the same valleys. The journey feels timeless, in that we are disconnected from our lives at home. And yet it feels as if we are but one page, or maybe nothing more than a single sentence, in a tale that began with Neolithic hunters walking beside this river, a story that will continue long after we float past.

The wild mooring stirs these thoughts. There is little else to do here but move slowly, think deeply, fit in.

Adapt.

Locks ... without bagels

So, I've been asked, just what is all this about canals and locks. Do they have to lock up the canals at night to keep them from being stolen? Not quite. Canals are mostly big ditches. We traveled north on the River Meuse, which was a "canalized river," meaning dams had been built to control the river flow and maintain its depth, with locks to pass you around each dam. We left the Meuse and turned west on the Canal des

Ardennes. That canal was dug using shovels and horses shortly after the Louisiana Purchase, in which France sold most of the Mississippi River region to the United States for three cents an acre. Back then, remember, before highways and trucks, pretty much before railroads, before paved roads, before much in the way of roads at all, the only efficient way to move goods from where they were produced to where they were used was by boat. Rivers were handy for boats but sometimes rivers went a tad wild and boats couldn't navigate them, and sometimes rivers just

didn't go where the business folks wanted the goods to go. The solution was to dig a ditch and to drag boats through those ditches.

That's a canal. A long ditch filled with water.

As in the song, "I've got a mule and her name is Sal. Fifteen miles on the Erie Canal." How's this for progress: fifteen miles would be a damn good day for us on the Ardennes Canal.

A fundamental problem came up when folks started digging these ditches: hills. Rivers flow where rivers flow because water flows down hill, and rivers wind and wend their way from up high to down low and eventually to the ocean. Digging a canal to go from Point A to Point B, however, could be a problem if Hill C happens to be in the middle. The solution, like so much else in the Middle Ages, came from an unexpected source.

Like spaghetti, like gunpowder, like cookies with little paper messages inside, the Chinese solved this problem with hills early on. They invented locks. Marco Polo brought the idea back from China. Leonardi da Vinci put down his paint brushes long enough to draw some canal locks, and, voila, Europe went through a public works project frenzy, with every king sending the peasants out to dig ditches and the royal engineers out to build canal locks. The locks HOOP DOET LEVEN squeezes through today are, in some cases, hundreds of years old but continue to work in basically the same way they did when first built.

Locks are like stairs that are placed every once in a while along the canal when the land goes up or down. Between the locks the water is level. At one side of the lock the water is at one level. At the other side of the lock, the canal is at a lower or higher level. The lock is the stairway between those two levels.

Locks have one fundamental rule: they are exceedingly cool. Go through your first lock and your reaction will be, "wow, that is exceedingly cool." Locks have no pumps, no hydraulic systems, no computers or electricity or much at all in the way of machinery (sure, some locks have been automated, but only to do the same thing that in other locks are done by muscle power). Here's a visualization of a lock. Picture an empty bathtub. Place your rubber ducky in the tub. It sits on the bottom. Turn on the water and fill the tub. The water rises. So does rubber ducky. Let it float around a while. Let the water out. The water level goes down. So does rubber ducky. Now picture a 70-foot, 65-ton 86-year-old canal barge in your bath tub. Everything else is the same.

51

The lock is a big bath tub with a pair of swinging doors at either end. When we approach a lock we tell it "we've arrived" and the swinging doors swing open. We motor in and tell the lock, "OK, we're inside now." The doors we came through swing shut. If we're going up in the lock, little windows in the uphill end doors open and water rushes in, filling the lock to the uphill level. Just like the rubber ducky, as the water rises, so does the barge. When the water in the lock is at the same level as the uphill canal section, the front doors swing open and out we motor.

Going down in the lock is the opposite. In we motor with the water at the uphill level. Windows in the far downhill end doors open and let water out of the lock. Down we go and out we motor, at the level of the lower section. You can play with this at http://www.pragmasoft.be/carnets/geo/ecluse/Ecluse.html and navigate the little boat through the lock.

Everything in the lock happens slowly. After you get past your fear of them, locking is calming, one element of the zen of barging, moving slowly, almost passively through the landscape.

Most days the locks are a long way apart, a half hour or an hour or even more between locks. Where it gets interesting is when the canal has to go up, or down, a hill. Leaving the Ardennes and entering into Champagne we went down a "chain" of locks from a high level down into a valley, 27 locks all within three kilometers, most of the locks just a few hundred feet apart. It was a long day to travel a short distance. We had dinner at 5:00 and went to bed by 7:30 that evening.

And it rained all day. The foredeck crew - Sandra - worked the wet, heavy ropes in the locks. The Captain - me - sat in the covered wheelhouse. Had to turn up the music when the rain on the roof got too loud. Such inequality caused the French Revolution.

Locks come in all different shapes and sizes. Which led to the embarrassing problem of a boat showing up at a lock it couldn't fit into. To get around this problem, the French government declared in 1879 that all locks would be built to a standard size, named for the minister of public works responsible for this concept, Charles de Freycinet. As a result, we mostly travel through Freycinet-sized locks: 39 meters long by 5.2 meters wide by 2.2 meters deep. The cargo barges we encounter, called peniches, have to suck in their bellies to fit these locks. To carry the maximum cargo, these Freycinet barges are all 38.5 meters long by 5.1 meters wide. Steering a peniche into a lock is like standing three feet back from a wine bottle and trying to toss the cork back in. HOOP isn't nearly that large, just 21.4 meters long and 3.9 meters wide. Watching a peniche enter a lock is an exercise in calm and panic. We're panicked. The husband and wife who operate peniches are calm. He's at the bow, cell phone pressed to an ear by his shoulder, cigarette in his mouth, casually tossing the mooring line onto the bollards in the lock side, all without looking up. She's at the wheel, driving into the lock, her cell phone held to her ear with her shoulder (are they speaking to each other, probably not), and, to complicate matters, a baby will be on her hip. They never touch the sides.

At first, we entered locks like a ball in a pinball machine, banging from side to side. But we got better. I'm at the wheel, turning it frantically to line the boat up with the sides of the lock. Sandra at the bow, ready to lasso the bollards (mushroom-shaped metal poles) at the sides of the lock. (Eventually, on the Burgundy Canal, Sandra got so proficient at lassoing bollards that locktenders greeted her as "la cowgirl.") She gives me the thumbs up sign to show she's tied on and I throw the engine in reverse to stop the barge before the front lock gates. Once the boat is stopped, I hop off and lift a blue pipe, which tells the lock to do its thing, emptying or filling, depending on whether we're heading up stream or down. We ever so slowly either rise up or sink down. When that is done, the doors in front of us open and out we go, heading for the next lock.

Not all locks are quite so automated. On the smaller canals, where we spend most of our time, the locks retain their original Rube Goldberg mechanisms for swinging the heavy metal doors open and closed, mechanisms with long arms or bars, some with large wheels or paddles to turn or push. The polite way of working these mechanisms is for the lock tender, the eclusier, to operate one side of the lock and for Sandra to work the other.

All thanks to some obscure Chinese engineer, whose descendant is now busily assembling iPhones and iPads for us to use on our barge.

Marooned

Lest this whole affair sound a tad too idyllic, I'll tell you about our first true life yachting adventure, reminiscent of our days hanging on in the high seas. We're long time sailors. Wind has been our Friend. Calm has been a Bummer. All that changed once we started motoring around in what is little more than a 70-foot, flat-bottomed steel shoebox. Sailboats have a deep keel projecting down from the center of the boat. Moving water is much happier meeting the skinny front edge of the keel than it is trying to push aside the wide flat side of the keel. That's how sailboats go forward even when the wind is pushing them sideways. And that's what all of our sailboats did, more or less. When the wind blew from the side of the boat you adjusted the sails, the keel bit in and the boat moved forward, at right angles to the wind direction.

Cool.

HOOP DOET LEVEN, our steel shoebox, is placidly content to slide through the water bow first, stern first or cabin side doors first. The big cargo peniches, of which HOOP in her younger days was a little sister, settle six feet into the water when they are filled with grain or sand or whatever. They take on water ballast when they have no cargo. Their entire flat sides become the equivalent of a keel. HOOP's only cargo is us, some furniture and several cases of wine. She sits high and proud in the water. In fact, the square footage of HOOP's side is almost exactly the

54

same as the square footage of the mainsail on our sailboat back home. As a result, when the wind blows from the side HOOP moves sideways.

Makes maneuvering interesting.

The day in question was supposed to be an easy hop from Berry-au-Bac, a commercial port where we spent the night with five big cargo peniches, to a small town just outside Reins, the capital of the Champagne region, home of a magnificent cathedral in which all the kings of France were crowned. Home to Veuve Cliquot, Pommery and Taittinger champagnes, among others. Just about 15 kilometers and nine locks. Four or so hours. Be there for lunch.

We woke to a downpour, but a windless one. That is do-able, more so for me in the wheelhouse than Sandra on the foredeck handling lines in the locks, but do-able. We'd had rain almost every day for three weeks. April showers, right? A cargo peniche had nestled in bow to bow with us in the evening, without our even noticing. His mooring line was on top of ours.

The captain, a young man, and his crew, a white German shepherd (canine, not human), were carrying the trash to a bin on shore. Sandra grabbed our trash and chatted him (them) up. He was leaving immediately, and commercial boats have priority over pleasure boats in the locks anyway. He casually flipped off his mooring lines and motored off to the lock. We waited for him to enter the lock and took off ourselves, planning a tricky maneuver going in reverse for several hundred meters then turning 90 degrees to port to enter the lock. Piece of cake. Even in the rain.

Except that the moment the mooring lines were free the sky turned black, the rain increased and the wind, the wind howled. The first victim of the blow was our intended reverse 90 degree turn to port (aka left). The wind preferred, instead, a 270 degree turn to starboard (the other left). The math worked out and we had no choice anyway so there we were, all lined up for the lock straight ahead. Problem was HOOP was moving sideways, across the face of the lock rather than straight into the opening. Lots of frantic wheel spinning, full forward, full reverse and, eyes closed, jam the throttle and bounce into the lock and there we were, maybe with a bit of painting required, but maybe not. We're well fendered.

Lock No. 1 of 9 completed, we motored off to Lock No. 2, just a few hundred meters away. It took two hours to get to it. When the lock appeared around a bend, there was Sandra's peniche buddy, and his dog, rising in the lock. We had to wait. Waiting turned out to be simple because the wind decided we should wait on the downwind side of the canal. We drifted to a stop, our tire fenders over the side to cushion the arrival. Oddly, though, there was a meter or so of water between us and the side of the canal when we came to a sudden stop. We were aground. OK, no big deal. We have two 15-foot wooden poles, barge poles, with medieval fittings on the end. Sandra uses a barge pole to lift mooring lines on and off the bollards in high locks. We also use the long poles to push away from some moorings, or away from the side of the canal when we stop for lunch. The idea is that you want to shove the aft end of the boat, where the propeller lives, into deeper water before putting it in gear. Protect your propeller is a key rule.

An hour later we were still trying to push the boat away from the canal bank against the wind. Sometimes we moved forward a bit. Sometimes backward a bit. Sometimes the prop and the engine moved us. Every time, however, the wind shoved us right bank onto the bank, and right back aground.

What to do? Call the Coast Guard for help? There isn't one. BoatUS (a commercial rescue service at home) would charge a fortune in mileage fees to get to us. Pas de problème. No problem. It was only 9:30. We hadn't had breakfast. We still had eggs Sandra had bought from a canalside farmer. An entire baguette remained in our bread bag. We had sacks of espresso. Breakfast. Canalside. The wind couldn't blow forever.

And it didn't. An hour or so later the rain stopped, the sun came out and the wind died down. We managed to pole away from the bank and headed for the lock, which had remained open and waiting for us through the whole affair. We pointed straight at the lock and, bam, the wind returned. With a vengeance. Bing, bam, pow and we rattled our way in.

This wasn't fun. The wind kept increasing. We ricocheted through two more locks then called it quits. We went through Lock No. 4 then tied up to the upwind side of the canal. That's where we sat for the night. Tied to our metal mooring stakes on the side of the canal. Surrounded by bright yellow fields of blooming rape seed. A church steeple in the distance. Not a person in sight.

Not quite a disaster.

Floating through Champagne

We spent a month floating through Champagne, leaving the rural Ardennes, home of dairy farms, forests and villages so small they lacked even a bakery (merde!). In one day we went from being tied up in the midst of fields, with the nearest town an hour's walk away, to motoring besides the highway and tying up in downtown Reims (rhymes with "France," somehow), the twelfth-largest city in France. We left the countryside, motored through what appeared to be an industrial suburb of Mordor and, voila, all of a sudden we were in the middle of a medieval city, passing the Cathedral where every French king was crowned. We felt as if

we were flying under the French radar at times like this, coasting into the city, tying up at the side of the canal and hopping off the boat to explore, all without being charged a euro. We paid more to park our rental car in Reims for three hours the prior year than to park our 70-foot barge for three nights.

Reims bills itself as the Capital of Champagne (but, then, so does just about every city, town, village and hut in the region). It is home to Taittinger, Pommery, Mumm, Veuve Cliquot and a dozen smaller houses. We toured Taittinger (pronounced "tay-tin-jay") and were duly impressed at seeing 10 million bottles sitting in underground caves carved by Roman slaves. But these big champagne houses are big business and slick and showy. The prior year, on the barge-shopping trip to nearby Epernay (which also bills itself as the Capital of Champagne), we visited Moet et Chandon and saw its 10 million underground bottles. You can't help but be impressed by anything on that scale. The Cathedral at Reims was equally huge, equally gargoyle-infested and instinctively infused us with two questions about building such a building: first, how in the world did they build something like that, then, second, why in the world did they build something like that? Cathedrals were the space program of the Middle Ages. Unlike the space program, though, they did not spin off world-changing goodies like Tang and Velcro and Teflon. Or light sabers, which I'm still waiting for. But I'm sure they impressed the masses and kept the stained glass artisans employed.

We spent a few days in Reims then left the city and motored out into the countryside to the town of Sillery, located at the foot of the Mountain of Reims, actually more of a hill, but oh so much more than just a hill. The slopes are where the champagne grapes are grown. Land there goes for a million euros an acre, when it goes on sale at all. Every village there, no matter how small, has, besides its boulangerie, tabac store selling newspapers and lottery tickets, and its hair dresser, a handful of champagne houses, none of which you will have heard of because none of their champagne leaves France. It turns out the Mountain of Reims is a half hour bike ride from the Canal of Sillery. Thusly was born the Rule of Buying Champagne: Always Buy from the Highest Vintner. You don't follow this rule because of some obscure oenological observation relating to air pressure or altitude infusing the grapes with bountiful bouquet. No, one follows this rule because a case of wine in thick champagne bottles is heavy. Coasting downhill from the Mountain of Reims to the Valley of the Canal did not require actually pedaling a pedal.

We followed the canal in an arc that took us to the other side of the Mountain of Reims, from the Reims side to the Epernay side, which happens to be the south-facing side. Every village on the south-facing side is quick to inform you when you enter that it is the "Capital of Champagne," because, after all, it is on the south-facing side. We settled in at Ay (pronounced "eye," probably because it doesn't contain a single letter "I"). Ay is across the Marne River from Epernay (remember, the Capital of Champagne). Epernay is slick and touristy. A trolley takes you from Moet et Chandon down the Avenue de Champagne past Champagne Perrier-Jouet, Bollinger and, of course, Dom Perignon.

Ay, however, is chock-a-block with literally mom-and-pop champagne houses. We picked one to visit: Champagne Pascal Henin. For comparison, at Taittinger we walked past underground vaults stacked with champagne bottles, aging away for year after year. One vault contained 72,242 bottles (a sign said so. They must employ a full time bottle counter). There were lots of those vaults at Taittinger. Pascal Henin produces 45,000 bottles a year, in a good year. But each of those bottles is blended by Pascal himself. So we visited the house where Pascal and Delphine Henin live. Delphine sat us down at the kitchen table and brought out bottles to sample. And sample. And sample. Pascal and Delphine started the business in 1990. They come from champagne families. As she put it, Pascal's family is pinot noir and chardonnay, the two primary grape varieties blended into champagne, but her family has the fields of pinot meunier, the third, and most subtle variety of grapes combined in various ratios to produce champagne. By their marriage, they literally became a blended family.

We bought a case containing their six different blends. This was too much for us to carry so, an hour later, our Champagne Pascal Henin was delivered to the barge by Pascal Henin himself, and son. I expect neither Monsieur Moet nor Monsieur Chandon do deliveries.

Champagne, on both the industrial and the familial scales, seems to be good business. The Ardennes was far from wealthy. The term "wealthy farmer" approaches being an oxymoron. Even in a Champagne village as small as Ay, however, the streets are literally paved with ceramics, glazed pottery cobblestones.

We kept promising ourselves we'd move on from Champagne and get the boat closer to Paris. It took a month, however. The weather was gorgeous. The countryside was gorgeous. And we gorged ourselves on champagne, which, we came to learn, is drinkable as any other wine and does not have to be reserved for New Year's Eve.

Feeding our addiction

Champagne was not all we had to drink. Within the geographic boundaries defining the acreage in which grapes can be legally sold with a "Champagne" label, land was too expensive to be used for anything but grape production. Outside that land of legal champagne, however, we were rarely out of sight of a cow.

Most were beef cattle. Many, though, were dairy cows. This presented an opportunity for us.

At home in Massachusetts our dealer provides high quality product to feed our addiction. A year before we left Massachusetts, the state government clamped down on our dealer and ordered her, in the typical legal manner of never using one word when two words meaning the same thing can be employed, "to cease and desist" from what it claimed were her illegal activities or face prosecution. What had been her under-the-table business morphed into an under-another-table-under-the-first-table operation. We continued to get good stuff. But what to do in France, where we had no connections and the law was murky? We gave ourselves a month to find a solution. We could last that long going without, we predicted. It took about six weeks to score, but score we did. Here's what happened.

But first, a clarification. Sure, we both may have inhaled in the Sixties (that's my age, not a reference to any particular decade), but our serious addiction is to raw, unprocessed, unpasteurized, unhomogenized, straight-from-the-udder-to-the-glass milk. White gold. Vin de bovine. Moo juice. Cream on top. In glass bottles. Milk in which after Bossie gets in the clover in the field, the milk tastes clovery. There is a cohort of true-milk believers at home, people with an almost religious zealotry about the benefits of drinking what they call "real milk" and the harmful effects of what they call "dead milk," milk that has been pasteurized to kill evil bacteria but in the process also kills beneficial bacteria. We've been drinking real milk for years. Sure, we could justify it by citing how we've avoided typhoid, beri beri, jaundice and Lyme disease since we started on raw milk, so it must be helping us, but there is a simpler explanation. I advocated for consumers when the Massachusetts Department of Agriculture tried to even further restrict access to raw milk. Following a milk-a-cow-on-Boston-Common protest, I was quoted in the Boston Globe as explaining why I drank raw milk. "Its like having ice cream for breakfast," I confessed.

The food safety laws in the European Union concerning unpasteurized milk are murky. Raw milk cheeses are permitted, under certain safety conditions. Raw milk sales laws vary from country to country. You don't see raw milk in food stores. Almost all milk, in fact, is sold in a form we don't see at all at home, unrefrigerated, ultra-processed into a form that lasts forever, more or less. We can usually find what to us would be normal, refrigerated – but pasteurized – milk hidden away in the store. But raw milk, never.

Until one rainy day when we were tied up in the village of Malmay, on the Canal des Ardennes, south of where the Battle of the Bulge was fought in World War Two. Malmay has just a handful of residents, a thousand-year-old Roman church and a top flight restaurant, where the special of the evening was a word we hesitated to translate, "pigeon." We woke to a chilly downpour. But we had our first guests on board, John and Linda from Portland, Maine. Linda had been a classmate of Sandra's at language school on the Cote d'Azur. Morning meant breakfast and breakfast, of course, meant croissants. I donned my raincoat and trudged down the road into the village, searching for the boulangerie.

Alas, Malmy had but four houses, a magnificent church, and the fancy restaurant, which was actually in the next village, Chemery-sur-Bar. None of the five residents were on the street. That is, until, like an apparition from a Tale of Two Cities, an old woman trudged through the downpour, a woman who I had seen in a dozen old, black and white foreign films playing the role of "peasant." She stared at me, who was neither Jacques nor Pierre, the two men who lived in town. Then she smiled and greeted me with a cheery bonjour. I offered what seemed to me to be a perfectly phrased question as to whether there was a possibility that this magnificent and beautiful village, which boasted such an ancient church and was located near a restaurant of international renown, might possibility contain a boulangerie. She looked confused and replied with my best known response, "je ne vous comprends pas," meaning, "I don't understand a word you are saying and I hesitate to even guess what language you are trying to speak." All was lost, alas.

But wait, all was not lost. In her gnarled hand she grasped the handle of a dented metal pail. A white towel covered the pail, protecting its content from the rain. Could it be? I asked, pointing, to offer a substitute means of communication, "Is that milk?"

"Bien sur," of course, she replied, pulling aside the towel and revealing the real stuff.

"Est que le lait cru?" Is that raw milk? I asked.

"Oui," she said, in a friendly and warming manner. This was becoming an interesting, or at least, odd conversation. She walked toward her house and opened the door.

I followed. "Where can one buy raw milk?" I asked, or at least I thought I asked. This caused an oddly puzzled expression to cross her face. Was this man an imbecile, she may have thought. Why is he bothering me?

"A la ferme," she mumbled. And walked into her house.

Now, this could have several meanings. She might have said that my thighs were firm and she was enticing me in for a glass of milk. More likely, however, "ferme" was a farm, and only an imbecile would think milk came from someplace other than a farm. That this second meaning was what she'd said was made more probable when she pointed down the road, where a house and a barn – and a tractor – were located. This was big. This could be the score. I thanked her.

I returned to the barge, sans croissants, but loaded with news. Sandra responded with passion, donning her own rain gear and, joined by Linda, trotted to the farm. She knocked on the door and was met by a burly man she'd spoken with the evening before, as he sat on his tractor. Can we buy milk, she asked. Of course, he answered and invited them into the kitchen, where his wife was at the table, a table that was what our "French Farmhouse Reproduction Table" from Crate & Barrel had been reproduced from, a table whose top was butter smooth from who-knew how many generations of meals. Discussion followed. Sandra and the woman walked to the dairy barn, where the cows had just been milked. Empty 2-liter plastic bottled water bottles were piled on a shelf. The woman took two bottles and dipped them - and her hands - into a tub of milk, filling them. She handed the bottles to Sandra and asked if she wanted any eggs. Bien sur, of course. The chickens were shushed aside and two dozen eggs were produced. They returned to the kitchen, where the farmer was showing Linda photos of their son, who worked on a nearby farm. Overlooking them from the wall was the mounted head of a tusked wild boar. The farmer proudly explained how he'd shot the boar. The head was on the wall. Three-hundred pounds of boar bacon was in the larder.

Back on the barge, the eggs were fried for our breakfast and we toasted our success with glasses of lait cru, real milk. Later that morning, we motored past the farm and received a big wave from the door.

Encounters like this happen constantly. They are the true adventure.

Stars and Stripes

May 8 was a good day to fly the American flag on HOOP DOET LEVEN. We'd wondered what flag to fly. Technically, the boat is registered in the United Kingdom and should fly a British flag, the Red Ensign identifying it as a British civilian vessel. That is what it flew formerly. But we felt a tad foolish pretending to be Brits, couldn't manage the accent or remember the words to Britannia Rules the Waves. On the other hand, there have been some uncomfortable moments in recent Franco-American relations (please don't force us to utter either "freedom fries" or "cheese eating surrender

monkeys" from the Simpsons). Nonetheless, we fly a rather large West Marine version of the Stars and Stripes from HOOP's stern.

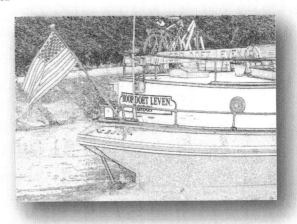

After a few years of barging we lessened the confusion of having a Dutch name on the bow, a London home port on the stern and the Stars and Stripes flying from a pole on the stern. With the help of a helpful Welshman (who suffers from an unfortunate lack of vowels in his name) at the British Registry of Shipping & Seamen we changed Hoop's home port from London to an obscure Lincolnshire fishing village called Boston. No need to specify just which Boston it now refers to on the nameboard.

We've never had a bad reaction to the flag. In fact, it has been just the opposite. It is surprising how often we are asked, somewhat stiffly, whether we are English. We respond with "no, no, no" (a word never said just once; one waiter educated us about the difference between saying "no, no," which means "no," and "no, oui," which for some reason means "yes") and say "nous sommes américaine," we are Americans. The questioner invariably breaks out in a grin and asks if we've ever been to New York, which to most French is the equivalent of the Emerald City of Oz, but with classier jeans.

For the past three days we'd been in Damery, a small town on the Marne River near the western edge of Champagne. We'd said over and over that we'd be leaving Champagne "tomorrow." It hadn't happened yet, almost a month after we'd arrived there. Damery, with a population of 1,300, has a dozen champagne production houses. We had lunch in a cafe on the river that day – ragout d'lapin, as in Bugs, as in the Easter one, as in the Velveteen one, and Peter, the Energizer one, Rodger, the Trix one, and, of course, the invisible one named Harvey – with a bottle of local Damery champagne. Our coffee cost the same as the champagne. Would you be in a rush to leave?

May 8 is VE day, the day the Germans surrendered in World War II. It is a big deal in France.

We'd planned a bike ride through the dirt paths in the vineyards. As we were getting the bikes set up an elderly man, carrying a metal rake, walked up to the boat and pointed at our flag. Speaking only French, he told us we were Americans. We agreed. He said he would give us a "souvenir" of Damery. "Souvenir" in French is more than a trinket, it means "memory". He said he was eight years old in 1944. The Germans were in Damery. One morning the Germans began blowing up the houses along the river. Then the bridge crossing the Marne was exploded and dropped into the river. American soldiers appeared on the far shore and started shelling the town. The Germans fled. Within an hour, he told us, the Americans had built a new bridge across the river "on top of boats" and for hour after hour tanks and trucks and jeeps drove through the town. It was General Patton's Third Army, he said. He stood by the side of the road when Patton himself drove past. He saluted. Patton returned the salute. The American bridge crossed exactly where HOOP DOET LEVEN was moored, he told us. Patton would have driven over our decks.

When he was finished I told him my father had been in France in the American Army and he had landed at Normandy. He shook our hands and said thank you.

Later, at noon, after our bike ride, all the town's church bells began ringing. We heard music and looked up at the bridge (the one that replaced the Marne bridge the Germans destroyed) to see musicians, soldiers, firefighters and a crowd marching across. We quickly joined the parade.

On the far side of the bridge were stone memorials to the First and Second World Wars. The band played, the mayor gave a speech, flags waved, everybody sang La Marseillaise, then they marched back across the bridge for lunch.

It was moving. Only a snail can fail to be moved by La Marseillaise (and snails have grounds for a personal grudge against the French). We'd travelled through historic military territory. The Meuse River, through Lorraine, was the scene of the worst of World War I trench warfare. Verdun epitomizes the senselessness of war, where the German strategy was to simply kill as many French as possible until they gave up the fight. The

Ardennes, where we travelled through lovely farmland, was the scene of the Battle of the Bulge, Germany's last major counterattack of World War II. We hadn't passed a hamlet without a war memorial covered with the names of the town's dead "enfants," its children. These memorials invariably have fresh flowers laid on them. Still

We live in an age where real wars can be difficult to distinguish from video games. Controllers in Colorado pilot drones over Afghanistan to bomb houses and cars, and sometimes weddings. A country song boasts "I can't tell Iraq from Iran." War is distant. Impersonal. We didn't even count how many civilians were killed in Iraq. America has wars on terror, on drugs, on poverty. But no living American has experienced war at home in America, has seen his home town invaded, bombed, burned, destroyed, neighbors killed, women raped. In France, especially in the countryside, the experience of war was real and remains real.

The ceremony in Damary reminded us of this. In addition, the flag on our stern and the visit from the man with the rake reminded us of the good that America did when it came to the defense of France. It was a good day, and not just because of the rabbit stew for lunch.

Taming nature, French style

It rained from our arrival at the beginning of March to the end of May. That isn't quite accurate. It did not rain at the end of May. It snowed at the end of May. People said it was the longest winter in France since 1917 and the winter of 1917 in France was as miserable as winter gets, for reasons not necessarily meteorological. The one word even I could understand in the weather forecasts was "inundation." But May came to an end and with that, winter, too, ended. Beginning June 1 and every day since it was hot and sunny, skies blue instead of gray, clouds white instead of gray, and our moods sunny instead of,

well, instead of gray.

The sounds of spring echo around us. Birds sing in a sexual frenzy, like 16 year old boys gazing love-stricken at girls' field hockey practice. Crickets do the insect version of singing, probably in the same sexual overload. Church bells chime almost constantly, making up for a winter's tintinnabulations that were drowned out by the roar of wind and rain. And overlying these bucolic sounds is the ever-present roar that is France at this time of year, the gently purring susurrations of . . . of . . . of . . . weed whackers. Months of rain followed by days of sunshine ignited anything green to burst forth in more of everything green. Stand in one place for five minutes barefoot and blades of grass will sprout through your toes. Linger under a bare tree in the sunshine and thirty minutes later you'll be shaded by 10,000 leaves newly generated. Mother Nature soaked in all that rain like a 48-year-old childless woman on fertility enhancement drugs, fearing that she has one last shot at fecundity, out came the sun and glory hallelujah, photosynthesis happened and Mom Nature shot forth with all she's got. If it was green yesterday, it is greener, and there's more of it today.

All France stood united to repel this invasion of undisciplined nature.

Groups of children cluster on sidewalks, staring into the distance, waiting for the government trucks to arrive, trucks that will deliver shiny weed whackers, roaring lawn mowers, scythes, rakes, hoes and other implements of destruction. No day is prouder than when a five-year-old French youth is handed his first tiny weed whacker, barely powerful enough to trim a blade of grass, or when a young girl tosses her dolls and EZ Bake oven into the recycling bin as she caresses her new mini-mower, always bright pink because France retains the blue-for-boys-pink-for-girls ethos well through the teen years. Boys and girls join men and women as each is assigned his and her designated spot of green to whack, mow, rake and subdue. This army prepares to set off for battle, then pauses, stymied.

Soon, though, the accoutrements van arrives. This being France, one does not, absolutely can not, just walk out the door and do anything without the correct accessories. Bicycle wheels fail to turn unless the feet on their pedals are shod in shoes specifically constructed for bicycle pedals so that when cyclists alight and attempt to walk to a cafe for coffee they click on the sidewalk and totter as if their ankles were made of wet noodle. Sandra, pedaling in her mary jane street shoes, draws a shocked silence. Fishermen stand on the river banks monitoring half a dozen fishing rods, confident that the fish swim from fisherperson to fisherperson selecting the man wearing the best woodland camouflage shoes, socks, pants, jacket and beret from whose hook to snatch bait. Men – meaning any male person over age four – dawdle for twenty minutes every morning selecting which scarf to casually drape around their necks before stepping outside. Street sweepers, men who literally sweep the streets clean with wood-handled brooms with a cluster of sticks tied to the street end, wear ankle-to-throat jump suits in day glo magenta, lime green and safety reflective yellow before stepping off the curb. I, too, "going native" as a fellow bargee alleged, wriggle into my double-zippered French blue coveralls before twirling a paint brush, cutting wood or launching into anything more workmanlike than brushing my teeth.

The Green Team is similarly outfitted: steel-tipped boots so they cannot amputate their toes with their whirling weed-cutting strings; not-in-the-least-subtle green jump suits accessorized with a dozen pockets and zippers, in shades to blend with Nature so the grass and weeds won't have time to flee before decapitation; plastic construction hard hats because, well who knows how swinging a weed whacker from side to side is likely to cause some hard object to drop from above; face shields to guard against flying grass blades scarring their cheeks.

As we cruise along the canal we see squads of these people – so heavily disguised and protected that their gender cannot be determined – slowly swinging their weed whackers from side to side, devastating entire fields and hillsides, a single field likely to require several days labor, a swipe at a time, working with the patience of those French fishermen who gaze at their fishing rods for hour after hour, knowing they are allotted but one fish per year. They work with the determination of bridge painters, certain that when they whack their way across the field, they'll have to trudge to the far end and begin again.

They work so hard. They smile and wave back when we smile and wave at them. They take their lunch at noon precisely and return to whacking everything green two hours later. And they do all this while assured that what they cut today will grow back tomorrow.

A skeptic would say this is all just make work to provide employment. But no, I've watched the eclusiers who push and pull lock gates open and closed for us while we apologize for interrupting them from their real tasks of whacking grass that encroaches within a quarter mile of the lock, I've watched the first thing these guys do when the lock shuts down for the day and they return to their locktender's houses for a well-deserved rest. What do they do, you ask? Open a bottle of Bourgogne? Slice a chunk of 18-month-old comte cheese to top today's baguette? No, no, no. Out comes the lawn mower and every blade of grass on their own locktender's cottage lawns runs for its life.

This is some French thing about controlling Nature. What goes for blades of grass goes double – no, quintuple – for Big Nature. Like for trees. Every Fall trucks roam throughout cities, towns, villages and communes, trucks with moving pneumatic arms like the trucks that repair downed power lines after the hurricane passes. These trucks, however, ignore utility poles, which are generally concrete in France anyway, but stop at every tree.

The buckets at the end of the pneumatic arms are stuffed with men, of course dressed in day-glo coveralls, waving chain saws over their heads like pirates leaping to board a Spanish treasure galleon. Within minutes every branch, yes, literally every branch sprouting from the central trunk, lies on the ground around the tree. A squad of these trucks leaves a street lined with what look like giant saguaro cactuses, stubs of arms, headless corpses. No leaves. No branches.

The first time you see these trees, standing naked and embarrassed, you wonder if this is a form of anti-public anti-nature graffiti, wanton destruction for the sake only of wanton destruction. Why doesn't the government do something about this, you wonder. And why do the men literally disarming and defoliating trees seem to be government employees? Is this some bizarre human Dutch elm disease?

No, no, no. This is France putting nature in its proper place, which is France, but properly accoutered and arranged. What happens is that once the randomness of trees is excised, what is left to grow dutifully grows where it is meant, meant by France herself, to grow. They are creating nothing less than full size municipal bonsai trees. What the Japanese do with teeny tiny scissors to create six inch high spruce forests to adorn their desks at the melting nuclear plant, France does with chain saws on thirty-foot elms lining main streets. And it works. By the end of the year these streets are lined with row after row of giant green lollipops, all identical in size, height, roundness. One variation involves leaving only branches that grow parallel to the street, excising those that grow toward or away from the street. Months later these streets are lined with trees that seem to be holding hands with one another, offering shade a street long and two yards wide.

This well-groomed attitude toward Nature is one of the harmless – unless you happen to be a towering chestnut tree next to the village smithy – quirks that make our wandering somewhat aimlessly through France so fascinating. Oh, but there are so many more such quirks.

One Sunday we took the local bus to the ancient town of Vitteaux, near the Canal de Bourgogne, primarily because it was supposed to have a great restaurant serving local food to local folks and an authentic flying saucer statue commemorating a recent visitation. We also learned that Vitteaux was known for, besides its central role in both French religious and extraterrestrial visitation history, its brioche, a breakfast pastry. Everybody has to be special for something and we had spent an entire winter in a city known for its onions. (When we tell people we spent the winter in Auxonne the general reaction is that French eye roll maneuver while muttering "oignons, beaucoup d'oignons.") Little did we know that it was not necessarily for the quality of its brioche that Vitteaux earned its place in the history books. It was size. In Vitteaux, size matters. It seems that on August 17, 1991, in the presence of Yves Lanier, president of the French bakers' Union Commercial and Artisanal, the world's largest brioche was baked in a specially constructed municipal brioche oven. This briochasaurus rex weighed 141 kilos (311 pounds) and was 3 meters (10 feet) in diameter. It required 1,100 eggs and, among other ingredients, 2 liters of rum. We know all this because not only has the world's largest brioche oven been preserved since its day of glory in 1991, but there is a detailed historic marker adjacent to the oven.

The flying saucer monument was a letdown. Fiberglass. Probably not a real flying saucer at all.

On the other hand, France does maintain its somewhat more legitimate historical artifacts. We rode our bikes to the medieval city of Semur-en-Auxois and spent the night at a hotel for Sandra's monthly mandatory bath, the booking of which taught Sandra the correct phrase to request a room with a tub: un chambre avec un salle de bain avec bain. Semur was straight from Hollywood's version of a medieval city with towering towers, ramparts, cobbled streets and a cathedral.

We wandered into the cathedral after dinner, drawn by the sound of a choir coming from inside and were awed by the acoustical mysteries of that favorite chant of Gregorian monks, Swing Low Sweet Chariot. The juxtaposition of a slave spiritual first sung in ramshackle plantation churches resonating through the glory of a medieval cathedral literally choked us up. Once again, the serendipitous mystery of France brought us to a standstill.

Finally, that week brought a solution to one of the mysteries of France that had puzzled me for the past year. I understand that in France mailboxes are square, not arched as in the U.S. and that they are most likely not "Approved by the Postmaster General of the United States," as every true American mailbox must declare on its face (the poor Postmaster General, sitting at a desk all day approving and disapproving mailbox designs.) I had never figured out why so many houses, especially in rural areas, have a long skinny tube on the wall next to their front door. French newspapers are not that dimension and, besides, I hadn't noticed any home newspaper deliveries, which would inhibit daily visits to the local tabac, the true source of important news. Then I saw a boulangerie truck jerk to a halt in a cloud of dust in front of a house next to the canal. Out leapt the boulangére, baguette in hand, AND HE RAMMED THE LOAF INTO THE TUBE. Voila. Mystery solved. The "second mailbox" is really the baguette box for those desperate souls who are unfortunate enough to reside in a town without its own boulangerie.

And all that, baguette delivery tubes, gospel in a medieval cathedral, uniforms for weed whacking and the world's largest brioche as a municipal project, are all parts, vital parts, of the mélange of France we've come to love.

European economic secrets

The economy. It is in the news and dominating politics. The U.S. economy. The European economy. Greece. Spain. France. Germany. Competing economic systems. Communism, where the government owns everything. Capitalism, where all property is owned privately. Socialism, where businesses are owned by the state.

And then there's France. We spent a day in a small town on the Marne not too far from Paris being introduced to the fundamental principle underlying the French economic system. It is called "brocants." A brocant is like a yard sale. Not for a household. Not even for a neighborhood. For an entire town. A yard sale in which everybody in town offers everything they don't want to everybody else in town, and to people from miles around. A year or so later, the same items get passed on at other brocants. Eventually, everything in France gets owned by everybody at one time or another. It isn't communism and isn't capitalism. It is more like Valentines Day in first grade, when everybody gives everybody else a card. More like musical chairs with property. Everybody shares everything. Serially.

Everything.

Anything.

We were introduced to the economics of brocants by our French doppelgangers (to mix European Union metaphors). Sandra and Harvey ("har-vee") met Sandrine and Herve' ("err-vay") in Dormans, a beautiful town on the River Marne. They were on HOOP DOET LEVEN one Saturday evening for drinks and invited us to join them the next day driving to a couple of village brocants. Their English was slightly better than our French. We communicated by sentences that seemed to alternate French and English. It was language school for all of us.

We leaped at the opportunity. Sandrine, it turned out, is the world's leading authority on brocants. She arrived fully-equipped with a folding cart stuffed with a pair of huge IKEA carrying bags for excess purchases. Herve' was our negotiator, cutting prices in half with a few deft words in French.

What made the brocant different from the flea markets we'd haunted at home was the communal nature of the sellers. The whole town cleaned out their cellars and toy cabinets and offered them for sale. Children sat behind tables covered with their trucks, dolls and outdated video games. Whole tables were piled with odd nuts, bolts, door knobs and broken tools. One woman proudly displayed dozens of carefully-knitted sweaters, vests, hats, jackets . . . for Barbie dolls.

We searched for movie DVDs, our nighttime entertainment on the boat. We have a French video player that won't accept U.S. DVDs. We need French releases of U.S. and British films that have sound tracks in both English and French. At the brocant, people gathered movies they'd become tired of watching and piled them on tables, all for sale. Herve' usually got the price to one euro or less. We bought a dozen. I scored the entire filmography of Twilight Zone, black and white and Rod Serling. I didn't think entertainment could get better than that until the man selling the DVDs told me about the best night of his life watching Alice Cooper perform in London.

Sandrine filled her cart with clothing, jewelry, and odd items that struck her fancy. She was fully dressed in items she'd bought at previous brocants and recited the incredibly low prices she'd paid for her necklaces, shoes and jacket. We wondered whether her home had turned into a warehouse for all the items she'd bought over the years. No, she told us, the Dormans brocant would be later this week and she would have a table there, selling items she no longer wanted.

This is how the French economy stays so active, as people sell what they no longer want to people who next want to own them, who then sell them in turn to new people. Children who outgrow their toys don't hide them in closets, instead, they pass them on to new children, who will certainly sell them to yet other children some day.

What a wise, and fun, and economical system.

But this being France, the brocant is about more than selling collections of champagne bottle caps or hand-made bird houses. It is about food. We had lunch in a double-decker London bus converted into a rolling restaurant. The key ingredient in my "Boston pizza" was crème fraîche, a delicacy far preferable to the baked beans people equate with the real Boston.

And as if the rolling restaurant were not enough, we idled with the Basque cheese man, who handed over slice after sample slice of his cheeses, sausages and jams, then, once we'd passed some key stage – still without buying anything – out came the liquors, sample after sample. We left with chunks of cheese and "sanglier," wild boar, sausages.

Then came the entertainment, dancers in what at first appeared to be some sort of native costume, red shirts and red skirts. The music started. The first cords sounded familiar. Edith Piaf? No, there was no accordion, just guitar. Ah, of course, Django Reinhardt, the French gypsy guitar legend. Wrong. The words were too familiar. "Heel-toe-dosey-doe / Come on baby, let's go boot scootin." Brooks and Dunn. Boot Scootin' Boogie. Straight from the Country Music Top Forty. A closer look at the "traditional French costumes" the dancers wore disclosed cowboy boots, ruffled shirts, Stetson hats and, could that be, yes, American flag handkerchiefs stuffed into the back pockets. They were line dancing. Alan Jackson on "Good Time" came next. Followed by, of course, "I've Got Friends in Low Places." Next was a favorite from Paris to Marseilles, "Save a Horse, Ride a Cowboy." This was more surreal than the Twilight Zone DVD.

We'll always have Paris

Just in front of the Ipswich (Massachusetts) Bay Yacht Club banner at our bow - most likely the only IBYC burgee flying at that moment on the entire continent - was Notre Dame Cathedral. We were most certainly in Paris. Almost two months after setting off from Toul. Paris.

Arriving in Paris, by barge, was interesting. "Interesting" is a highly nuanced word when it comes to boats. Back when I was learning to fly gliders my instructor explained how landings can be judged by degrees of moisture. There are dry mouth landings, moist armpit landings and soaked pants landings. (No such thing as a "crash landing," he said. Crashes and landings are two distinct events. One you walk away from, the other, well, use your imagination.)

"Interesting" boating events are similar to that concept. If you survive, its interesting.

Fortunately, our arrival in Paris never got beyond being interesting.

Coming down the Marne river with the spring floods had also been interesting. Sometimes we passed entire trees floating down the river. Sometimes the trees passed us. Most "interesting" was that the engine tended to run hot, as in once in a while the temperature gauge would start climbing, climbing and climbing and I would desperately look for a place to tie up the boat before the engine totally overheated. Some days at my morning engine checks the engine coolant level would be down a few inches and I would have to top it up. I was used to tiny sailboat diesel engines, small enough to fit in a suitcase. HOOP's six cylinder Ford diesel has a room of its own. I'll confess that it intimidated me.

Especially when we passed the intersection where the Marne flowed into the Seine, just a few kilometers upriver from Paris. The two rivers, both enhanced by the heavy spring rains, joined into an "interesting" torrent. With my prone-to-overheat engine I was dreading becoming a tourist attraction as my 70-foot engineless barge careened from historic Paris bridge to historic Paris bridge.

But we weren't planning on going too far into Paris, at least not on the barge. The plan was to turn off the river at a lock leading to the Canal St. Martin, five kilometers from the Marne-Seine junction, just before Notre Dame. The principal Paris marina is located just beyond that lock at the Paris Arsenal, a train station closed in 1939 so railroad employees could be shipped off to repel the Germans; it never reopened. The Marina is at the former moat that surrounded the Bastille. We continued past the Arsenal, however, another 4.5 kilometers up the Canal St. Martin to the Bassin la Villette for the Dutch Barge Association (DBA) rally with 35 other barges. That sounded doable, even with our hot tempered engine.

The entry to Paris could hardly have been more dramatic. After a month traveling down the River Marne we went through a giant lock, holding four barges at the same time with room to spare, and joined the River Seine just upriver from the city. Each day for the past few travel days we'd shared the river with larger and larger commercial vessels. On the Seine we were passed by what looked like ocean-going ships unloading cargoes at terminals on both sides of the river and then, as we entered the city proper, tourist boats – called bateau mouches; a "mouche" is a "fly" – buzzed past us on both sides. Together with the Batobus, large passenger carrying boat-buses filled with tourists. But we motored on, looking for the small lock on the side of the river that would lead into the Arsenal marina. We were intent on the right river bank, looking for the lock, when Sandra looked to the left and shouted: "Notre Dame."

We followed the directions we'd been given - turn right just before the Notre Dame Cathedral. Ho hum, just another ordinary day. Working our way off the Seine and through the lock and then through the Arsenal marina, we motored into a long, partially-lit tunnel that marked the beginning of the Canal St. Martin. Talk about the French Underground. This 2 kilometer tunnel took us underneath the streets of Paris. Above us was the Place de la Bastille, the site of the Bastille fortress stormed on July 14, 1789 as the start of the French Revolution. Sunlight streamed through round openings in the ceiling of the tunnel. We could hear traffic above us. Birds flew through the openings and back out into the sunlight. Eighteen minutes later we reached the end of the tunnel, went through a lock and there we were in the 10th Arrondissement of Paris, busy streets on both sides, cars whizzing past us, the canal banks filled with people having lunch, shops on both sides and a barrage of food smells from restaurants and bakeries. We motored on through four pairs of double locks. Bridges lifted for us, lock doors swung open and we floated higher and higher into Paris. All in all, we went through nine locks in the middle of urban Paris. Like driving a 70-foot boat down State Street in Boston. People waved and shouted, taking photos. Sandra chatted with watchers at every lock. Cars drove past on both sides of the boat.

After an hour we reached the Bassin la Villette, a wide area in the 19th Arrondissement at the convergence of two canals in the middle of a Paris neighborhood of shops, apartments, restaurants and parks. We found our place with the other barges attending the 20th anniversary rally of the Dutch Barge Association and completed the transition from being the only boat on the Rivers Meuse and Marne for week after week in April and May, to one of 36 barges — far from the largest — tied up four deep in the middle of Paris.

As if this experience were not bizarre enough - driving a boat through the streets of Paris - it turned out to be the weekend of the Queen's Diamond Jubilee, the 60th anniversary of Queen Elizabeth II's ascension to the throne. The mostly-British DBA took this event seriously. After all, the highlight of the London celebrations would be the Queen cruising down the Thames in her own royal barge, accompanied by an armada that would include representatives from the DBA itself.

The Queen's subjects were instructed to celebrate along with her in a Big Jubilee Lunch wherever in the realm they happened to be. Including Paris. The barging Brits we were moored with did their part. A wandering French choral group was convinced to serenade us with appropriately patriotic tunes and we all joined in with a rousing version of God Save the Queen, you know, the ditty that uses the same tune as our My Country Tis of Thee song.

To avoid confusion, I hummed along, trying not to be too distracted by the New Zeelander sitting across from me laughing hysterically, repeating, "God Save the Queen. They're singing God Save the Queen. Haven't heard that since third grade. God Save the Queen. Ha ha ha."

We spent five days in Paris. High on our shopping list was finding a couple of spare tires to add to our collection of tires-on-a-rope to dangle over the sides whenever a stone wall approached us at a faster rate than we approved of. Not a typical tourist purchase. And, in the end, one better saved for shopping outside the city.

Paris, of course, was fun. But we couldn't wait to get back under way. Back into the countryside.

Back someplace where I could figure out why our engine was overheating.

Finding Fontainebleau

The dividing line between a long vacation and a lifestyle change is far from clear, as with so many dividing lines. (I once had a business client who told me that my job as a lawyer was to tell the client where the line was between what was legal and what was not, and then to tell him just how thick the line was so he could push his toes against the far edge of that line. I told the client to keep his shoes on and just do the right thing.) However, there are some pretty good indicators of when you have gone beyond the limits of a vacation. The second haircut away from home is one indicator. Buying shoes to replace the ones you've worn out. Changing the battery in your watch. Receiving a notice from the post office that the period for forwarding your mail has expired. And, of course, the killer indicator, giving a two-year lease on your home at home.

We'd passed all those landmarks. After four months it was obvious we were not on vacation. We'd moved to France. Changed our residence. Changed our lives. When asked a question we responded with "oui," rather than "yes." We bought a baguette every morning, and fed yesterday's leftover crusts to the swans because who would eat day-old bread? We flushed the boat's toilet by pressing a button and barely remembered those lever things. Most of all, the social lubricants changed. Rather than grinning ferociously at everybody on the sidewalk, you respected their space. On the other hand, you never leapt into any transaction, at a store, on the street, in a restaurant by just saying what you had to say. Instead, you eased in with a bonjour, with a comment on the weather, with a Madame or a Monsieur or, if both are together, with a single word contraction "monsieurdame," accompanied by the appropriate nodding of your head.

A slow moving checkout line was not cause for aggravation but an opportunity to meet the man in front of you and the woman behind you.

Most of all the difference between a vacation and a lifestyle change is the matter of time. Vacations have an end, a definite day by which you will return to real life. Whatever is to happen on vacation has to happen by that time. We had a target for returning home – maybe permanently, maybe not – but it was so far off that it was not, yet, a factor, not, yet, real. Instead, we were at the stage where when we motored the barge into a new town we didn't know whether we'd leave in the morning or stay for a week. It depended. And we might return there next year, or never again.

Our trip to Fontainbleau was an example of this. We'd left Paris, happily, after overdosing on The Big City, and were working our way up the Haute Seine, the portion of the River Seine that goes beyond Paris. The river there is wide and swift, filled with large commercial barges lugging sand and gravel to city construction sites. The river banks are a mix of expensive vacation homes for wealthy Parisians, ultra-modern homes that are more glass than walls, and homes with towers and turrets and whimsical outbuildings that attempt to emulate medieval chateaus in miniature. Somewhere in the midst of all this is the town of Fontainebleau, where the kings of France had their summer hunting lodge and palace, and where Napoleon spent most of his time when he wasn't out conquering the world. It has been fully restored, the only royal residence in Europe returned to near its original, ostentatious state. Well worth a visit.

So, we decided we'd visit Fontainebleau. Our canal chart showed a port for Fontainebleau on the Haute Seine. We pulled in to a marina there. The problem was our 86-year-old Dutch barge, 70-feet or so long, wasn't a "marina" sort of vessel.

"This feels wrong," Sandra declared as we lay bouncing against a flimsy aluminum dock, standing out like a circus fat man at a fashion model juice bar. "Lets get out of this place."

"Sure, it feels wrong, but not too wrong," I replied, a tad smarmy. This was a marina. We were in a boat. That was good enough for me. Then the aluminum dock our 65-ton barge was tied to creaked - and possibly, maybe in a barely perceptible way, started to bend and buckle. I was convinced.

"OK. I'm convinced," I said. The vibe was wrong. We untied our mooring lines and moved on. This isn't something that can be done on a vacation, when schedules and well-laid plans predominate. Take One at Fontainebleau was a flop.

We motored on up the Seine until we came to the next lock. We'd learned that both upriver and downriver from these large locks on the Seine the waterways authority had built long walls for commercial boats to tie up for the night. We could snuggle up against the far end of these walls without interfering with the huge commercial barges, like the mice in the horse barn, and spend a night. We did just that at the next lock, in Champagne-sur-Seine (which has nothing to do with the bubbly wine), and tied ourselves to a wall between the largest boats we'd yet encountered. Stayed three nights. Free. The town had two boulangeries selling bread and croissants, and a small market in which the sole clerk carefully sniffed every melon in his bins until he found just the right one for us to buy, addicting us to the boule de mielle, the "ball of honey" melon.

Google Earth told us this town was no farther from Fontainebleau than the marina we'd fled from. We planned a bicycle expedition. The next morning, after unloading our two bikes from the aft deck, Sandra fell into conversation with an older man walking his dog along the river bank. Eventually the conversation turned to our plan to ride to Fontainebleau. What is the best way to get there, Sandra asked.

"Ah, Fontainebleu," he said. "Ooh la la." Only in France can a man, a gnarly, old man, get away with saying ooh la la. The man's eyes lit up and, simultaneously, his French sped up.

He pointed up the river. Follow the Seine that way, he told Sandra, who was struggling to keep up with his accelerating vowels. Then turn off onto the River Loing. Go to the ecluse, the lock, and cross over the barrage, the dam. Then just go a droit, a droit, a droit. Straight, straight, straight. (Not to be confused with droite, droite, droite, which, to my ears, sounds exactly the same but means right, right, right. See why we kept getting lost in France.)

That seemed like a rather nautical set of directions for a bike trip and, on further inquiry, it turned out he'd spent his life delivering "farina," grain, in his barge, on which he still lived. He was a Frenchman who knew his rivers and canals, but the rest of his country was as much terra incognita as the far side of the Hudson River is to native New Yorkers. They know it exists and possibly people of some sort live there but they certainly don't know anybody who has actually been there.

Nonetheless, or maybe simply because of his barge connection, we followed his directions, riding our bikes along the towpath further up the Seine, coming to the junction with the River Loing, riding down to the first canal lock and over the dam and then riding straight, straight, and even more straight, ending up - somewhere that was most certainly not Fontainebleau.

But it was an interesting place, a village surrounded by stone walls, across an arched bridge over a river, with a tower and a gateway and arrow slits and all the accoutrements of medieval architecture.

The town of Moret-sur-Loing. Not a king's summer residence, certainly, but the home of a Benedictine convent that from 1638 to 1972 (when the nuns moved to Paris) used its secret recipe to manufacture Sucre d'Orge, barley sugar candy. And Napoleon did spend a night there. And I had my first escargot, triggering a compulsion that sends snails racing away from me ever since, as fast as they can slither, which, of course, is far from fast enough. So, we ended up spending a whole day in Moret. Take Two at Fontainebleau was not quite a failure, but not quite successful.

The next day we just took the train, a 10-minute ride to Fontainebleau. It was all it had been billed to be, over the top gaudy, room after room after room of gilt and brocade and splendor and ego, surprising us with just how short Napoleon's bed was, not that size matters. If nothing else, Fontainebleau explained, and justified, the French Revolution.

The point of this is not to discuss how superfluous the heads of French kings were but, rather to focus on the difference between a vacation and a change in one's life. You can't spend three days of a vacation trying repeatedly to see one "attraction." But because you can't do that you miss out on the serendipitous events that take place when time is not an issue, meeting the Frenchman whose country is limited to what can be seen from the waterways, receiving a lesson in melon ball sniffing, spending a day at the home of Benedictine nuns with a 450-year sweet tooth, or simply succeeding through perseverance.

Patience. Time. Serendipity. All gifts from HOOP DOET LEVEN.

Gifts from France.

Keeping a close watch on the market

We've learned that in this time of financial instability, living in retirement and getting by on what we've squirreled away during our working decades, it is vital that we pay close attention to the markets. Not the stock market. That has treated us as kindly as a nasty neighbor obsessed with our tree limbs swaying over the fence line. No, in France the market we track is the local marche', or to be more precise, the marche' en pleine aire, the outdoor market. Most towns have a market day. The larger the town the more market days it has. Reins (remember, rhymes with ". . .") has a marche', someplace, every day.

We tied up for several days at a lock about twenty miles outside of Paris, just passing the time. We were surrounded by trees, fields and the wide river beside us. Peniches, the large commercial barges, hustled past us, those traveling en aval (downstream) furiously slowing to enter the lock just below us, those en amont (going upstream) churning foaming wakes as they accelerate from a standstill to a crawl, out from the lock. Our first day resident there we tried to ride our bikes to town for groceries. As we passed the lock, though, the eclusier waived us over. He'd drive us into town, he said, leaving us to wonder what happens to barges arriving at the lock while he was giving us the town tour for an hour. In return, Sandra walked his two dogs, who, not surprisingly, would immediately sit at her feet in response to "assis au pied." Incroyable. All the dogs here speak French, or at least understand it.

Our second day was the market day in the next town upriver from us, Lagny-sur-Marne. We unloaded our bikes from the aft deck, strapped on our panniers and pedaled eight kilometers along the flat pathway next to the river. Lagny, we'd been told, has a great marche'.

But first, lest I wallow idyllically in the quaintness of everything French, I have to note that France is chockablock with super-duper-supermarkets, and I'll confess that we spend our share of time, and euros, at them. The day after our arrival at the boat in Toul we were shown the way to the local Cora market and were blown away with the variety of what it sold, from flat screen Samsung televisions to Giant (pronounced "gee-ont") Verte canned green beans (as in "ho ho ho from the Valley of the Giant Verte"), from Old El Paso tortillas to foie gras, lawnmowers to fresh bread, plus four aisles – four long aisles – of wine. Different versions of these stores, and the French clones of Costco and Home Depot, are common. And they are crowded. And the prices are pretty good, although a liter of Coca Cola and a liter of Bordeaux cost about the same.

But what is fascinating about France is how easily these anonymous 21st Century institutions – each with the individuality and charm of a McDonalds – rub cultural shoulders with as medieval an institution as the marche' en pleine aire. Farmers have been carrying their products to the same market squares in these towns since the days of the Black Plague, since before the Crusades, probably since before Roman legionnaires were the first unwelcome tourists to visit here. They sell what is in season. We waited too long to visit the local strawberry farmer's table and the best were snapped up by the time we returned. The man selling preparations from tomatoes and olives and spices and nuts chatted with us, in English, between customers, seeking assurance that Obama "and not that other person" would win the election.

The woman cooking crepes introduced us to her grandmother. And Nutella.

The marche' has one cheese vendor after another and, we've learned, cheese comes in grades. Supermarket cheese is better than we get at home, but only the desperate buy it rather than from the fromagerie at the marche'.

Steaks are the smallest part of what the butchers sell, rather, it is their own sausages and pates, dried, smoked and cured meats that fill their displays.

Outside the food area are stalls selling everything from toys to buttons to shoes and dresses, books and tools and even a truck with sides folding down to reveal an array of mattresses.

The marche' is as much a feast for the nose as it is for the eyes, ears and, of course, taste. Besides the spices and the baked goods, the platters of paella and prepared foods to go, there is the powerful aroma from the rotisserie chicken trucks, trucks in which a side folds down to reveal row on row of skewered chickens rotating in front of gas burners, juices dribbling from the highest to the lowest and down onto the potatoes resting in a pan on the bottom. You point to a chicken and the roti man stuffs it into a sack and spoons in juices and potatoes. We get three meals from one of these chickens, and usually get to chat with the farmer who raised it.

The marche' is an experience. After stuffing our bike bags we sit at an outside table sipping coffees and watching people. The table is ours for as long as we want. We could have stayed for lunch — and dinner. The entertainment at the cafe is free: all of France walking by, or sitting at the next table. Us watching them.

Them watching us.

Sounds French

We were deep into Burgundy. The Canal de Bourgogne was built 200 years or so ago by either Italian or British prisoners of war, depending on the guide book. One version has the canal's three-kilometer tunnel having been dug by British prisoners of Napoleon, who were lowered into the tunnel from above and given their freedom when they dug their way out. It is a narrow, shallow canal, used only by pleasure boats. We pushed its limits, both for water depth below and for clearance in the tunnel above, with our barge. We woke up one morning heeled at an angle reminiscent of our sailing days, sitting on the bottom, leaning against the bank, the result of an overly eager lock tender letting too much water drain from his section of the canal over night. But it is beautiful here in what one reference called "the quintessential France," rich in sights – rolling hillsides along both sides of the canal – and tastes – vineyards dropping down to the water's edge and snails crawling through garlic, pesto and olive oil. Running for their lives.

But what got our attention here was not the sights but the sounds of France. Once in a while, when the barge is motoring past wheat fields to port and acres of sunflowers to starboard, when the sun is shining and a breeze is blowing (but not so much that entering a lock is an exercise in biting the inside of your cheeks and waiting for the sound of 87-year-old iron crunching into 200-year-old stone), when you sit on the bench at the bow, looking around the bend in the canal for the bow of an approaching boat, you are so deeply into France and all things French that you hear a faint rhythm that in Scotland would be a bagpipe but in France has to be an accordion. Ah, this is what all the planning and worrying was about.

But other times, this place can get on your nerves with sounds as soothing as chalk squeaking on a blackboard (not that anybody actually uses chalk any more, or, come to think of it, not that they even manufacture blackboards any more). Sometimes all you seem to hear are noises as soothing as a slowly dripping faucet at 3:00 a.m.. Some examples:

Church bells. OK, what kind of person would complain about church bells, you ask. Is he going to moan and groan about bird songs next? (Wait a moment, that comes soon). Church bells. Every village in France has a church. Sometimes all it takes to be a village is a boulangerie, a hairdresser – for both femmes and hommes – a pharmacy with a flashing neon green cross to serve a populace of hypochondriacs in a country where the government pays for all their medications, and a church, the older the better. Sometimes all of the above plus a pet groomer – for both chiens and chats – in which case the town earns a second church. And maybe a third one if in 1350 or so there was a wealthy patron who couldn't tolerate either local priest (which brings to mind the joke about the Jewish sailor shipwrecked on a desert island – and what is a "desert island" besides an oxymoronic cliché – who is rescued after twenty years. When his rescuers ask what the three shacks are that he built during his exile the sailor says that the first is where he lives, the second is his synagogue and the third is the synagogue in which he wouldn't be caught dead.) So, wherever you happen to be in France you will likely be within sight, and sound, of one, two, three or even more churches.

And what is the problem with that, you inquire. Every church has a bell tower. Every bell tower, has, duh, a bell, or several bells, and a clock. If they all rang at once, the result would be a cacophony rather than a symphony. Each church, it seems, wants to be the soloist. The result, one theorizes, is that every church prefers to be the one church, or at least the first church, to inform its parishioners of the correct time. Over the years, over the decades and centuries, this has led to an arms race, or more accurately, an ears race, in which church clocks have been nudged a minute or so faster every once in a while so Saint Here's bells will ring just a minute or two before Saint Somebody Else rings. Of course, Saint Somebody Else can just as easily give it's minute hand a twitch or two forward. The result, after century after century of this tempero-audio one-minuteupsmanship is that most church clocks in France are several weeks, or months, fast. Add to this phenomenon the custom of ringing the hour – sometimes all through the night – plus bonus chimes every fifteen minutes to mark the quarter hours, plus seemingly random musical flurries from time to time, and, as if that auditory avalanche were not enough, add the universal practice of churches repeating the hourly ring at five minutes after the hour just in case Jacques had been gargling at the precise hour and had not heard the chimes, what has resulted is an auditory status of complete randomness. At any given moment in any given location you are likely to hear a bell ringing, a kind of national tinnitus. A little bit of bell ringing goes a long way. In some towns, the bells never stop.

For those with sufficient obsessive compulsive disorder to be incapacitated while a clock chimes because each chime absolutely must be counted, this situation becomes disabling, made all the worse by what is apparently some parishes refusal to recognize the existence of daylight savings time so that the count of one church's chimes differs from the next church's chimes three minutes later.

Most bells at least sound, well, bell-like. A few, however, sound like budget bells, purchased at the foundry's annual close-out sale. I won't mention any church in particular, but should you happen to be in Tonnerre in Bourgogne in the afternoon and should you have any sort of musical sensibility, your only consolation will be that French churches uniformly refuse to switch to the 24-hour time the rest of the country uses.

That's the problem with bells.

Birds. So what's to complain about with bird songs? That is my mother's fault (yes, Doctor, you were so correct that everything is my mother's fault). In her constant quest for "cultchah" Mom came home one day with a windup cuckoo clock, the kind with the little door that swings open every hour to eject a little bird who goes "cuckoo, cuckoo, cuckoo" to mark the hour, one "cuckoo" for each hour. Imagine a seven-year-old boy lying awake on his bed at 3:00 a.m., struggling to keep his eyes open so the nightmare of space aliens, or leaches, or monsters under the bed will evaporate, counting cuckoos through the night. Cuckoo, cuckoo. One, two. Then an hour later as the eye blinks last longer than the eyes jammed wide open comes cuckoo, cuckoo, cuckoo. One, two, three. Etc. A few years of that and OCD counting is as automatic as breathing.

Fast forward fifty-seven or so years. Same boy, but now sleeping the well-earned sleep of the recently-retired. Its 3:00 a.m. and through slumber and eyes sealed shut by French fairy dust comes the blast of "cuckoo, cuckoo, cuckoo." Sleep-sealed lips whisper a silent "une, deux, trois." Followed by "cuckoo, cuckoo, cuckoo, cuckoo, cuckoo." "Four, five, six, seven, eight." Then, immediately, "cuckoo, cuckoo, cuckoo, cuckoo, cuckoo." "Nine, ten, eleven, twelve, thirteen." Eyes slam open. Thirteen? In the middle of the night? What gives? "Cuckoo, cuckoo, cuckoo, cuckoo, cuckoo, cuckoo." Something is obviously wrong. Seriously wrong. But the cuckoos must be counted. Twenty-eight, twenty-nine, thirty.

I haven't heard a real living cuckoo bird in the States (although Audubon-addicted friends insist they exist, four North American species of them). Who even knew there were real living cuckoo birds. The only place they seemed to exist outside of clocks was in cartoons, where they flew around the heads of cats that were smashed on the noggin with mallets by malevolent mice.

But in France cuckoo birds, real birds, feathers, wings, the full bird thing, are scattered through the countryside. Those Swiss, or Japanese, clock makers who manufactured Mom's cuckoo clock got their "cuckoo" sound down pat, an impersonation worthy of a Las Vegas act at a clockmakers' convention. Every week or so, at random moments of the day, or more commonly, the night, seemingly perched on the wheelhouse roof comes "cuckoo, cuckoo, cuckoo," followed, silently by "seventy-five, seventy-six, seventy-seven." The French must eat cuckoo au povre, right? Sounds like a grand idea.

We know why they eat frogs. At some rural moorings – need I mention the beatific location where we spent six nights tied up next to the historic Forge de Buffon (the French equivalent, for you on Boston's north shore, of the Saugus iron works, but a tad classier) our boat is besieged through the night by bullfrogs doing impersonations of ducks with sore throats, choking on clumps of stale bread while sneezing through hiccups. Sound unpleasant? After a few hours this chorus makes you want to tear off their slimy green legs and gnaw on them.

Hmm, perhaps with garlic and oil. Could this be an explanation of the basis of French cuisine? Eat whoever annoys you.

Wonder when we'll hear the plaintive love call of the lonely snail.

Masters of our own fete

Brace yourself. Overly Vast Generalization Alert. Out it comes: "The French know how to enjoy themselves and generally have a better time than Americans." That's my story and I'm sticking to it. And here, Your Honors, is Exhibit A in support of that proposition.

June 21, the Summer Solstice, the longest day of the year. I'll bet that if you happened to be in the U. S. of A., the event passed with nary a fanfare, probably unnoticed, nothing special. Did you have loads of fun that day? Do you even remember what you did? Well, we had a blast, so good a time that while we usually pop awake at 6:00 a.m., we both slept until 9:00 the next morning, truly teenage waking times.

We had a blast because so did most everybody else in France. June 21, the longest day of the year, is cele-

brated in every French village, town, commune and city with the Fete de la Musique, a national musical extravaganza in which anything goes – musically that is – and every musical instrument in France is expected to toot, strum, pluck, roll, pick, pound, tap, jingle and otherwise do its resonating thing. Our first French Fete de la Musique we were in Reins, the Capital of Champagne, on our way to check out a barge called HOOP DOET LEVEN. We pooped out early, after overdosing on enthusiastic garage bands so loud they'd been evicted from their garages. A year later we were in Joigny, a large town on the River Yonne at the northern edge of Burgundy. Purely by coincidence, and as a result of flooding that closed the canal we intended to be on, we were back in Joigny exactly a year later for our third musical extravaganza. Joigny remains medieval. The new buildings – with ornate carved wood facades on the houses – were built after a fire destroyed much of the town. In the 16th Century.

I liked the Joigny town flag, which flew from many buildings. The flag featured the official town seal with two crossed wooden maillets, long-handled wooden mallets, which were used by grape harvesters to bang the bungs into the wine barrels. The town symbol doesn't symbolize winemaking, but rather a 1438 rebellion of the town's Maillotins – the mallet-bearers – who used their mauls to, well, to maul the lord of the manor to death.

The entire town turned out at sunset for the Fete de la Musique. We joined in. Walking over the arched bridge we met the local ladies' choir, young women, old women, in-between women, all having a blast singing French folk songs to the folks sitting at tables on the plaza or wandering by.

Walking up through the packed streets, we encountered a rock band competing with two women playing accordions. The rockers were far louder, and well-amplified. The determined accordion women outlasted them, however, and, in the end, prevailed, displaying rather smug smiles at their victory.

People wandered the streets with instrument cases on their backs. A blues band played in front of the covered market building. Sidewalks were packed with tables from the cafes, bars and restaurants. Children danced. Old men danced. Drunks danced. Even one American tourist couple, who, after an accordion woman insisted they looked like they came from Ireland, loudly declared – with volume compensating for their absolute lack of a single syllable of French – that "no, we're from New

Jersey," even they waltzed to an accordion tune. A man who Sandra said looked quintessentially French played his flugelhorn.

Just as we thought the musical spectrum was exhausted, from up the street, in front of the town's cultural center once again came those fundamentally French rhythms we hadn't heard since the brocant on the River Marne. Wandering up the hill past a row of 16th Century wooden houses, down another hill from the 12th Century church in front of which the lord of the manor was mauled, were the local ladies wearing swirly skirts, cowboy boots and Stetson hats. The local line dancing society. And they had the largest crowd of all.

Can it get any weirder than that? perhaps. The ZZ Top tribute band played last month.

Downhill from here

Its all downhill from here, more or less. We'd been climbing since Paris, meaning that on rivers we'd been traveling upstream against the current and in canals we'd been entering the locks at the low water side and getting lifted up, then exiting at the high water end. We'd climbed a water stairway from Paris up to the high point – on the waterways at least – of Burgundy. We reached the peak at Pouilly-en-Axois, the entry point to the 3.5 kilometer Pouilly Tunnel. As the hills got steeper, the locks got closer together. In our last three days of climbing we'd passed through 45 locks. One day – a day with 30 locks – we traveled just nine kilometers in nine hours. It keeps your attention, with the next lock literally within sight of the previous one, but it is fun, and satisfying, exercising our newly learned skills. We'd passed through our 350th lock of the summer by the time we reached Pouilly-en-Axois.

We'd been through a few tunnels before this one, but Pouilly had been lurking in our future for a few months. It would be the first tunnel with a ceiling so low that we had to dismantle the boat's wheelhouse and lay it flat on deck to fit through. The wheelhouse, the wood structure where we steered the boat from, was designed to be lowered to fit under low bridges and tunnels. The roof was made from three lightweight panels that lifted off and stored on deck. The front and back of the wheelhouse were hinged and folded down flat, forwards and back. The sides lifted off.

In the old, pre-motor days, bargees would lie on their backs on top of their barge and walk their feet along the tunnel ceiling to propel the barge through the low Pouilly tunnel.

Lowering the wheelhouse and motoring through the well-lit tunnel all sounded simple enough but since we'd never actually gone through the process we were a tad apprehensive. We left ourselves plenty of time, not planning on transiting the tunnel for a couple of days after our arrival. As with most things on the French canals, such well laid often get misplaced. The canal authority's usually laisez faire attitude toward actually enforcing its hundreds of regulations makes an exception for the Pouilly tunnel. Before we were given permission to go through the tunnel, the lock tender came on board and checked that we each had a life jacket and that we had a spotlight. Uncharacteristically, he even went so far as to check whether the spotlight worked, making me turn it on.

We were to learn why he was so efficient. Good thing we gave ourselves plenty of time to prepare. This sounded serious.

It sounded especially serious when the day before our planned passage, with the wheelhouse still in place, because it was raining, the lock tender strolled by and told us we'd be going through the tunnel in 45 minutes. He gave us a very good reason for this sudden change in plans. At least I think it was a very good reason. Once we understood that we'd be leaving in 45 minutes, both Sandra and I lost any further ability to understand French.

We did figure out his parting words.

"Les lumières dans le tunnel sont brisés aujourd'hui." The lights in the tunnel don't work today. The lights don't work. It wasn't August when nobody works in France. Or Monday, which is still the weekend. Or Thursday, which is almost Friday, which is just before the weekend. But, nonetheless, the tunnel lights were taking a day off. For three kilometers (1.8 miles). Underground.

What doesn't kill you, or totally embarrass you, makes you stronger. We survived the darkness.

And the bats. In the darkness.

And we'd gotten permission to tie up right on the other side of the tunnel. So we could put the wheelhouse back right away. In the rain.

Except that the locktender on the starting end hadn't told the lock-tender on the ending end we would be tying up there for the night. Instead, just about the time we pulled up next to the sloping grassy bank on the far side of the tunnel, at exactly the moment Sandra leapt from the barge toward, but not quite up to that sloping grassy bank, splashing into the canal, in the rain, the far end locktender puttered up on her motor-bike asking us what we were doing. What Sandra was doing was dragging herself from the canal up the grassy bank, soaked through from the shoulders down.

The locktender either failed to notice that Sandra was in the canal, or, more likely, the locktender was too polite to question why she had gone swimming, fully dressed, mooring line in hand, in the rain. In any event, we were told they were prepared for us to continue on, down through nine more locks, to Vandenesse-en-Auxois. Four VNF lock-tenders were standing by to speed us through, we were told.

And speed us through they did. The four locktenders, women college students, were mounted on motorbikes. They worked in pairs, leap-frogging one another to prepare each lock for our arrival, opening the lock gates so we could enter without pausing. Our flying angels, we called them. It was a speedy, wet trip, through the rain, with the wheelhouse folded down.

And Sandra mopping all the way.

But it was downhill, that day and for the next few weeks, 55 locks dropping us through Burgundy toward our next big city, Dijon, the mustard capital.

One of our guidebooks called Bourgogne "the quintessential France." This section of canal was the quintessential Bourgogne, meaning, among other things, that the villages were sparse and the chances to buy groceries more sparse. We travelled slowly, not that we had much choice with a canal speed limit of 6 kilometers – that's 3.6 miles an hour – and a lock to navigate every twenty minutes or so. With a few exceptions – such as the 900-year-old castle at Chateauneuf, meaning the "new castle" - all we see are farms after farms after farms.

We went day after day without fresh bread, the precise human rights deprivation, you may recall from French history, that triggered the French Revolution (Marie Antoinette, remember, responded to moans of the peasants that they had no bread with her famous reference to eating cake instead). We'd been warned about this side of the slope being tres tres rural, as opposed to the other slope, which was merely tres rural. There are few places to buy provisions, we'd been told.

We resorted to eating frozen bread. See, barging can have its hardships.

The sunflowers eased our struggle. Burgundy wine country lay ahead of us. On this stretch of canal we motored through sunflower country. On both sides of the boat sunflower fields reached as far as we could see. They'd just blossomed, eerily blossomed over a single night, sprouting yellow heads by the millions. If sunflowers were Martians, we'd be heading for the hills. We speculated that they would be used to make sunflower oil. There can't be that large a market for those miniscule plastic sacks of salted sunflower seeds. And the world supply of vases could not hold all the stalks we see at any given moment.

With a week before the grandkids – and their parental units, to utilize a Coneheadian term – arrived we tied to our metal stakes on the banks of the canal, shaded by a row of poplar trees that line the tow path. A million or so sunflowers were outside the window, backed by a just-plowed field, its red earth soil reaching down the valley in the distance. We were in the midst of a French heat wave, not the most comfortable place to be inside what is essentially an iron shoe box. The barge bakes in the sun and we spread various canvas shades, awnings and umbrellas over as much as we can, waiting until noon, when the tree shade covers us. We ran low on everything except cheese. Inside the refrigerator a Roquefortian miasma swirled, not altogether unpleasant, but making for interesting and none-too-subtle flavors permeating everything else we ate, except the shell-protected eggs.

Finally, low on provisions, we decided to ride our bikes down the towpath and find a market. Our 1992 canal guidebook told us comfortingly that when Bill Clinton was first running for President, a village 12 kilometers down the canal had a "small grocery." Perhaps it is still there. Right, and perhaps it has a swimming pool filled with cool water and friendly dolphins. We mount our bikes – the cleverest purchase we'd made in France – and pedal down the canal tow path (which sounds better in French: chemin de haulage). Canal towpaths make fine bikeways, as the Bourgogne Regional Tourist Authority reminds us, incongruously, at every canal lock, with brightly colored signs extolling the joys of pedaling from village to village at speeds so rapid as to snap your head back so you stare at the clouds as you take your first stroke on the pedals, at least compared with the barge, which, when you shove the throttle forward makes all sorts of impressive engine noises, shoots funnels of diesel fumes from the exhaust and, like the coyote in Roadrunner cartoons, takes thirty seconds of all this fuss before beginning to imperceptibly inch forward.

But the tourist board has it right about biking along the canal. The tow path, on which horses – and, sometimes, barge wives – used to drag canal boats, runs just a few feet from the water's edge. On this canal the paths are well maintained, hard packed stone and sometimes even black-top. Because of the intrinsic nature of canals – water remains level from lock to lock – the tow paths are flat. Only at the locks is there either a small up or a small down, for fifty feet or so. This is followed by more of absolutely flat and level until the next lock. It makes for simple and pain-less cycling. An hour's cycling takes us as far as a day's barging. We often ride ahead to check out overnight mooring areas.

Well, our promised grocery store must have expired just about the time Bill Clinton met Monica Lewinsky. We couldn't find the market. We couldn't find the village in which the market was supposed to be located. This was far from a tragedy. We'd come to expect that every disappoint-ment on the canals simply opens the door to a new surprise.

In one cluster of houses in which the market also did not exist, which we'd searched on our way down the canal before pedaling onward, we'd seen three tables on the sidewalk in front of a menu board. On the ride back to the boat we heard a clock chime twelve times (followed, since this is France, by another church clock chiming twelve times ten minutes later, and another, faintly in the distance, five minutes after that). In a country in which tractor trailer trucks pull off the highway at noon because, of course, it is time for lunch, in which even automated lock gates won't open between 12:00 and 13:00 (French for noon and 1:00 p.m.), we could not expect our bicycles to function during that interreg-num. We stopped at l' Etape ("the Stop," appropriately enough). Yet again, we had a French restaurant experience.

The three sidewalk tables were in the hot sun so we sat inside, watch-ing the Olympic torch being rowed down the Thames on TV. French television adores such British pageantry, although the stunning French television correspondents struggled - unsuccessfully - to control their smirks at British pomp. The restaurant was staffed, in its entirety, by a hard-working young woman. Her husband-boyfriend-father-employee, somebody, must have inhabited the kitchen, but we never saw him. As with many small restaurants, the chef decided what we would eat that day, a selection called the "menu." That word has somewhat different meanings in France and the United States. We think of the "menu" as everything a restaurant has to offer, the full diverse selection. It sort of means the same thing in France. Sort of. But the "menu" is the only thing offered that day. You get one of each: first course, second course, dessert (or cheese). Coffee is extra but who would not have coffee after a meal. Each day's menu includes an "entree," which is not what Americans consider to be an "entree" – the main course – but in France is what comes first, as in the "entry" to the meal. The French "entree" is the American "appetizer." The "menu de jour" includes an "entree." The chef decides what the day's entree will be. After the entree comes the "plate," the main course. At l 'Etape today the "plate" was a pork roast, "roti porc." Take it or leave it. Want lunch there today, that was what you ate.

It was fantastic. The entree was a selection of pates, made that morning in the kitchen, grated carrots in oil, potato salad doused with creme fraise (my road to riches will be to become the North American creme fraise czar, everything, shoes included, tastes better smothered in creme fraise). Pickles, olives.

The roti porc (what we'd spell as "pork") led us to violate our general inclination against French pork, not for religious reasons but more because while we see beef herds grazing in the fields and chickens in the yards, we've yet to actually see any French pigs, leading to a suspicion that hogs don't live wild and crazy lives here. And along with the bowl of porc was a kettle of the best pomme frits we'd had here, quarters of potatoes with firmly roasted skins, sprinkled in herbs, not a spot of grease on them.

This was a meal in which every item, smallest to largest, had been prepared that day at the restaurant by monsieur in the kitchen, nothing prepackaged. It had been cooked with care, with thought, with skill. It was not fast food or junk food or standardized food constructed from a chain restaurant's food preparation manual. We compared it with a story about a British bargee's experience at a Texas steakhouse in which he ordered his steak "medium" and was told they were out of medium; all the steaks were pre-grilled.

The point of this food discussion is not to extol French cuisine; everybody knows French food is excellent. And there are some things France stumbles with. Properly managing a continental, multi-national economic and political union, for example, comes to mind. But there are other things, matters that actually impact citizens' lives directly, that the French walk through with comfort and grace. Food is one of them. This lunch was at a restaurant that for all appearances was a two-person operation, in a village so small it lacked a grocery or a boulangerie. How much business could it do in a day? Yet what it did it did with class, with care, with skill, with excellence. How rare it is to encounter that at home.

Lunch was that day's cadeau de France, a gift from France. We never found the grocery store and had to excavate in our freezer for dinner, but we spent our two hour lunch watching the Olympic torch and working our way through the entire menu at l 'Etape. It was a pleasant and civilized conclusion to the heat wave.

But we had to correct one misunderstanding. On the way out the door, not quite looking forward to the pedal back to the boat after such a lunch, we spotted a small sign in the window. We'd been wrong about the day's menu being all that was available. Monsieur le chef also made pizza.

The fishing lottery

Wherever we are on the rivers and canals, from downtown Paris to the isolated stretches of the Ardennes, we are rarely out of sight of a fisherman. This tropism toward dangling a hook in the water could be the only common characteristic of French socialists and South Carolina farmers. Walking from the barge to the boulangerie requires elbowing aside hordes of men holding fishing poles along the river banks. Poissonneries – fish markets – are rare. We buy our fish either at the Friday public market or the hypermarchè (pronounced "eeper-mar-shay"), one size larger than a supermarché.

First, though, excuse a digression into the traps of the French language in regard to fish matters, one that has snared me repeatedly, especially in restaurants. There are, at least to my American ears, no differences in pronunciation between "poisson" – a fish – and "poison" – meaning the same as in English.

This can lead to raised eyebrows from waiters speculating as to my emotional well being when I order a toxic dinner. Similarly, should we, or especially Sandra, casually ask a man holding a fishing rod on the river bank whether he likes to pêcher, pronounced "payshay", meaning to fish, she'll elicit a different response than if she asks if he likes to pécher, pronounced "pishee", meaning to sin. Fish matters are slippery, even before any creatures aquatic emerge.

But back to fishing in France. I come from a fishing community. Nearby is Gloucester, Massachusetts, setting for Kipling's novel "Captains Courageous" and the just as wonderful 1937 movie version with Spencer Tracy and Freddie Bartholomew; home (before he was sold from Gloucester to General Mills, then to Unilever, and now to Nippon Suisan Kaisha, Ltd. of Japan) of the famous Gorton's fisherman. I fish from time to time, although when I carry my fly rod through the saltmarsh in our back yard down Greenwood Creek, where submarine-sized striped bass lurk, Sandra asks what kind of pizza I want for dinner. Friends at the Ipswich Bay Yacht Club spend goodly portions of their summers chasing stripers and bluefish. A fishing expedition with my favorite dentist on his lobsteryacht takes us to the secret coordinates of fish heaven, a location he elicits, I expect, by placing professional Gloucester fishermen under just the right dosages of soporifics while filling their dental cavities. Fishing expeditions, after the cost of fuel, food and beer, yield cod and flounder at $20 to $40 per fish. So I've got nothing at all against fishing, and I recognize that when looked at through a financial lens, the optimum method to get a plateful of codfish is to visit the supermarket. I acknowledge that fishing isn't necessarily and entirely about just catching a fish.

French fishing, at least the freshwater variety we see along the rivers and canals, is all about equipment and accoutrements. Picture your typical Bourguignon fisherman from the ground up. Knee high rubber boots, what we would call "wellies," after the Duke of Wellington, who defeated some guy named Napoleon at the Battle of Waterloo; the French, presumably, have a different term for these boots, out of national pride. (As a further digression, besides having rubber boots named after him, the Duke is also the namesake for Beef Wellington, tenderloin and truffles in a pastry, although there is some speculation this overcooked beef dish is actually named after the rubber boot rather than the duke. In any event, the Duke is challenged in the military/culinary terminology realm by the Chinese General Gau (or, at some Chinese restaurants, Tsao), of chicken fame. Why don't modern military leaders gain similar culinary fame: Schwarzkopf Grits, Patraeus Paella, Shalikashvilli Shishkabob?)

OK, sorry about that. Wait, one further digression. Even Napoleon has a pastry named after himself, of course. The Napoleon, which, mysteriously, is not called a Napoleon in France itself, but is called a millefeuille, meaning "a thousand leaves," for all the layers of butter infused pastry dough it requires. This is among my favorite pastries. Unfortunately, it is also among my top three most difficult words to pronounce. The "mille," meaning thousand, part is simple. Pronouncing "feuille" requires exercising facial muscles that have lain dormant my entire life.

OK, back to fishing. Picture your French fisherman: knee high rubber boots topped with a full camo outfit, pants, jacket, hat. Camo belt. Underwear, probably. While I recognize the purpose of camouflage clothing for hunters and special forces soldiers, why fishermen dress in camo is a mystery. Do fish really stare up through the surface of the water spying on humans? And if they do, considering the angles involved, wouldn't sky-colored clothing, with cloud-colored accents, be a better disguise?

Sometimes the French fisherman will wear a long apron over his camo. Presumably to keep the fish blood from soiling his camo.

One fishing rod is rarely sufficient. Most French fisherman simultaneously deploy a minimum of two but usually three or four fishing rods in a variety of types. Most common are four-meter poles that disassemble into four or more segments, without reels, just a line attached at the end. In narrow canals when they see our barge heading toward them they retract their rod a segment at a time to let us clear. In addition he will have the usual spinning and casting rods. This assortment is mounted on what is actually called, in French, a "rod pod," a rack that holds all four rods side by side, each with their lines in the water. He will always have a net on a pole, and a net tube going down to the water to keep bait fish alive. A shelter, ranging from a simple umbrella to elaborate tents must be erected. Lures and baits are changed constantly. Folding chairs, often folding tables, are set up. The rods remain in the rod pod during lunch, but a wine bottle invariably sits on the table.

A dog, or two, is mandatory.

While we see men fishing from boats from time to time, most fishing is done from shore, but rarely just by standing on the canal bank itself. The canals and rivers are studded with fishing platforms extending out from the bank, from shaky constructions of random sticks and planks to elaborately built concrete and steel platforms.

This being France, not only must each fisherman be licensed, but also each fishing platform, with its registration number prominently displayed.

And this being France, river banks in cities and towns have regularly-spaced municipally-constructed fishing platforms. Interspersed among the municipal platforms are reserved handicapped-accessible, ramped platforms for wheelchair-bound fishermen, marked with signage restricting them to the disabled.

The riverbanks are marked with signs establishing the variety of restrictions placed on each section: no fishing area, fishing-only area, night-fishing area, no night-fishing area.

Of course, American fishermen go to just as extreme lengths in terms of their outfits, both sartorial and apparatus. And Americans can certainly be just as obsessed with their quest for fish. Just check out the Bassmaster web site: www.bassmaster.com. First prize for catching the largest fish is $500,000. For a fish. An uncooked fish. Seven Texas women were recently indicted for violating a Texas felony statute prohibiting cheating in fishing tournaments – they stuffed fish with ice and lead weights to make them heavier. The law carries a penalty of up to 10 years in prison. Prison. For the equivalent of spreading their hands just a tad too far apart while describing their catch.

OK, so why make such a big deal about French fishing? Is there something fundamentally different between fishing in the States and fishing in France?

Well, there is one little item. Based on observing hundreds, perhaps thousands of French fisherman as we passed by them day after day after day after day, there was one thing we never, with less than a handful, an amputated handful, of exceptions, ever observed at the end of a fishing line, the end not attached to the fisherman himself. That one thing missing was:

Fish.

We see fish jumping in the water all the time. We look into the water and there they are, sometimes teeny tiny, sometimes far larger than would fit in an aquarium. Once in a while true fish monsters.

But the fishermen never seem to catch the fish. Sure, one time, early on in April, I saw a man kneeling on the bank holding what looked like a catfishasaurus rex while his buddy took a photo. From time to time I've seen somebody remove a minnow from his hook, although whether it was a fish he caught, using an even smaller minnow, or a bait fish he'd placed on the hook by hand we never knew. Otherwise, the fishermen remain on the river bank and the fish remain in the river. Is there something French fish know. Or that French fishermen don't know? Its a mystery.

Does this vast expenditure of money, time and effort for so little reward indicate something about France?

I think it might. Fishermen at home expect to catch a fish with some frequency. It doesn't always happen and there are, from time to time, totally dry days on the water. But that is the exception. In France, dry days on the water appear to be the norm. The odds of actually catching a fish of any appreciable size seem closer to winning the lottery than to just a good day of fishing. So why do so many Frenchmen spend so much effort for so little reward? All I can do is speculate. Certainly the pleasure of being outside, in nature, is a reward. But that pleasure diminishes as the rain and cold increase, and neither snow nor rain nor heat nor gloom of night deter the fishermen. They just hunker down, bait their hooks and stare at the water, wiping the rain from their faces from time to time.

Solitude isn't the reason. While the norm is four fishing rods per fisherman sitting alone on the bank, sometimes that is reversed and what I see looks more like a construction site with four men watching the fifth hold a fishing rod gazing at the water. It isn't even to get away from the wife. She'll often be there standing stiffly on the river bank, waiting patiently, holding her pocketbook, while her husband baits his hooks.

Its a mystery.

So if bass fishing tournaments with $500,000 prizes and felony statutes with 10 year imprisonment penalties for fraudulent fishing indicate anything about America, then fishing with lottery odds of catching a fish says something about France. But what it says I just don't know.

But, then, I don't quite understand why millions of people spend good money on lottery tickets with equally infinitesimal chances of winning.

Dijon - yes, we can spare some Grey Poupon

We transitioned from the countryside to the city at Dijon, a city of about 250,000. What Pittsburgh is (or once was) to steel, what Boston is to baked beans, what New Jersey is to _____(fill in the blank depending on the ordure of your last Garden State encounter), well, that is what Dijon is to mustard. Mustard, the ketchup of France. Just as Reims "(the champagne capital") has vast underground caves crammed with millions of bottles of bubbly, one suspects that underlying the medieval city of Dijon are ginormous vaults into which are pumped lakes of yellow mustard.

Dijon is a charming city. After six weeks of rural Bourgogne, however, any place with a traffic light took on a fair amount of attraction. A place with not only traffic lights but choices of bars, cafes and restaurants, a place that sells pants to fit my shrinking waistline, a place in which if one boulangerie is closed ("But monsieur, of course we are open seven days a week, but not today, today is Tuesday") then the one next door will be open, Such a place, whether or not it is "the mustard capital," gets our attention. Dijon, however, is more than mustard. It is the former capital of the Ducs of Bourgogne. Ducs aren't "ducks," although in Dijon the barge was surrounded by what appeared to be a rare breed of nocturnal barking ducks, but the French spelling of "Dukes," as in the "Dukes of Hazard," but with more class and fewer souped-up Pontiacs. The Ducs of Burgundy. Back when Burgundy was its own nation, back when this slice of what is now France also included the Netherlands (acquired as the dowry of a Dutch princess marrying a Burgundian duc; imagine the desperation of her parents to be willing to toss in their entire country as an inducement to take their daughter off their hands), Dijon was the capital city of a country as politically powerful as its neighbor, called "France." Its medieval downtown is chock-a-block with 800-year-old timber-framed buildings, churches and palaces.

Palaces, statues and mansions of the various ducs abound: Phillip the Bold, John the Good, John the Fearless, Robert the Old and Mary the Rich. Makes you wonder how these ducs received their honorifics. Did they get to choose their own titles? They could not have been bestowed on them at birth, or at their assumption of the ducdom (see, for example, Robert the Old). You can't help but be impressed by the perspicacity in distinguishing between Phillip the Bold and John the Fearless. In any case, any of these titles is preferable to the Transylvanian king Vlad the Impaler. Or the manic-depressive Charles VI of France, variously called Charles the Mad and Charles the Beloved.

We went on a guided walking tour of historic Dijon and enjoyed it so much we returned the next day for a walking tour of Dijon gastronomy, which was mainly about mustard, with a bit of spiced bread ("similar to the spiced bread in Reims, but we use better wheat") and an introduction to Kir, the Cassis liquor named after a former mayor of Dijon, a "mad monk" who adored the drink. Kir, we were told, should only be sipped undiluted, except when it is added to white wine or, even better to champagne (a "kir royale") or it can be dribbled over ice cream. And always buy the bottle with the highest alcohol content, the sign of quality. Buy square bottles rather than round ones. And drink it within a year or it goes bad. That is everything you will ever need to know about kir, except why a "mad monk" ever became mayor of a capital city.

But mustard was the main attraction. We went to the Maille mustard store, the major mustard manufacturer of Dijon, before a certain Monsieur Poupon (the "Gray?") made an offer to Monsieur Maille that he could not refuse. We did our first (and most likely, last, after all, how many of these can one do) mustard tasting, carefully dipping little tasteless baked swizzle sticks into small mustard pots and commenting on the distinction between mustard vin blanc and mustard Chablis ("slightly fruity with a hint of chamomile, would go well with, let me think, yes, a Fenway frank"). The highlight was watching people bring in their mustard pots to be refilled at the mustard fountains: three taps offering a selection of mustard vin blanc, mustard Chablis and, of course, the original recipe, mustard anciens.

Not a jar of Guldens in sight, and surprisingly, not a bottle of French's mustard in the entire city.

Culture clash

A week before our grandsons Noah and Abram, and their parents Ben and Carolyn, were to arrive for a couple of weeks, our hot water heater - referred to on the right side of the Atlantic as a "calorifier" - gave up the ghost. Too bad. It was a glorious brass cylinder that bore no identifying marks and was most likely hand crafted by some handy craftsman in England, perhaps, or maybe the Netherlands. In any event, what had been dark pit marks covering its sides burst forth as full fledged holes. No combination of caulking goop or duct tape staunched the flow. It was time for a new calorifier before two teenaged boys, soon to be sweaty from operating canal lock gates, arrived.

Fortunately, we were meeting the family in Dijon. Just two days down the

Canal de Bourgogne was Saint Jean de Losne ("the Barge Capital of France"). Our big event in Saint Jean de Losne, besides the Saturday night concert on the quay by a mostly-Michael Jackson mostly-tribute band – "Billee Jean eez not ma lov-aa" – was that Blanquart Marine was able to get us a new hot water heater to replace our dead, antique one in just two days, In France. In August. Of course they could not install it – "but it is August, monsieur, there is nobody to do the work" – but we managed to do it ourselves and we had hot water again. So we set off onto a new canal, the Canal de Rhine au Rhone, which doesn't really connect the Rhine with the Rhone River.

We motored on to the city of Dole, which, just as did Dijon, boasts that it was the "Capital of Burgundy." It is the birthplace of Louis Pasteur. We checked out the "humble" house in which he was born and found it not so humble. After all, the Pasteurs had far more room to roam than we do on the barge. We learned that after he discovered germs he inaugurated the now-universal French practice of wrapping newly-purchased baguettes in paper. The boys were more than pleased with Dole. We tied to the quay next to the Bateau Pizza a seemingly permanently moored – it has a mailbox – barge with a brick chimney for its wood-fired oven. Seven nights a week it turns out pizzas. The guys worked up their courage for a pizza bourguignon: tomato, parsley, cheese, olives and escargots

This was their first trip to Europe, or much out of the United States, except for Canada and a week on the catamaran in the Abacos on our last nautical escape. As teen and pre-teen boys will do, their talk, and thoughts, were dominated by sports. Noah missed the first week of football training. For him, culture clash meant deciding whether to keep his lacrosse "flow" – the long curling locks that are supposed to flow from the back of the lacrosse helmet – or join the other guys on the football team in shaving his head. Lacrosse and football. Two opposing cultures. France doesn't figure into that equation.

Who knew that lacrosse was far more than a sport, but a culture, and style, unto itself. Off-field lacrosse clothing includes lacrosse-themed shirts – "May the flow be with you" – and long, bright, baggy shorts. The guys' mission for this trip was to "introduce" France to lacrosse culture. Any introduction of the actual sport itself was stymied by the U.S. Department of Homeland Security, which, in its so-far-successful campaign to block Ojibway and Huron terrorists from hijacking airliners, bans lacrosse sticks from carry-on baggage. The government is to be applauded for this insightful position, although the mechanics of an actual lacrosse-assisted hijacking are difficult to picture. "Flight attendant, tell the captain to fly this plane to Baltimore before the Hopkins game starts or I'll cross-check you, cradle my way to the cockpit, and drive a goal shot through the windshield."

In any event, all that made it to France was the après-game lacrosse wear, which certainly succeeded at turning French heads. After all, it was not black but long and baggy and exceedingly bright. UnFrench.

France struck back. In a big, way. More accurately, in a small way. We gave Ben and Carolyn the day off to explore Dole and have a leisurely cafe lunch. We took the boys to the Aqua park ISIS (I would not be surprised if in the intervening years the water park has changed its name), with water slides, Olympic pool, the whole kit and kaboodle, the French simulacrum of the Water Country in Portsmouth, New Hampshire, near their home in Dover. Sort of. Lacrosse-wear met French-wear, aqua-style. The guys stepped out of the changing rooms in full lacrosse-fashion regalia, ready to rock, roll, splash and slide. They weren't quite sure what to expect from a French water park, not sure, due to a Schwartz family legend, one of those stories that gets better with the retelling (see the reference to our official Poetic License, and recall our daughter Nicole's innocent question to me before we left home: "Are you excited to go to a continent where nobody has heard your stories even once yet?")

Here's the Family Legend, condensed version. Some time in the late 1980's, my parents rented a condo in Cannes, on the French Riviera, for the summer. Various permutations of the family flew over to spend time there. Ben was about 13 years old at the time. The French Riviera being what it is, or at least, what it was, the beaches were an interesting place for a young lad facing the full hormonal geyser young lads live through at that age. The Legend, part I, has it that Ben spent all of his beach time lying on a towel on his stomach, wearing sun glasses while surrounded by a parade of topless women, mostly older, at least to him, women. Interesting, and a story to take home. But wait, the story gets better. The elder Schwartzes, as with the present permutation, knew that a little France can go a long way for young guys. There was a water park in Cannes. There we all went. And there IT happened. We did the water slide thing and then perched in beach chairs to watch the happenings. Young Ben, a handsome lad, as he is now, but with more hair, was sitting in a beach chair, a 13-year-old young man watching the passing scene, when two French girls, just his age, just the age of the girls in his school, girls who but for the happenstance of where they were born could have been in homeroom with him, looked him in the eye, stood in front of him, wiggled as 13-year-old girls are just learning to wiggle – they were 13-year-old French girls remember – reached behind their backs and unhooked their bikini tops, letting them drop to the ground as they ran into the water. Laughing. Only Ben can say whether he has ever fully recovered.

That's the Legend of French Water Parks. The boys knew that legend. What they did not know was what would happen at the water park in Dole.

Well, THAT didn't happen, not at all. The guys strutted out from the changing room in their full lacrosse-wear glory, shorts to their knees, tee shirts declaring something about their favorite sport, to be faced by a hoard of French flesh, no bare breasts, but lots of flesh, boys in Speedos, girls in what looked like Speedos with tops, older women, large older women, wearing just what the girls were wearing, men, older and far larger men, wearing Speedos, probably, if you could lift their bellies and look underneath. In short, in very short, lots of French flesh on display, all running and jumping and splashing and jiggling.

But no lacrosse-wear. No short, or long, pants of any kind. Nothing reaching the knee. Nothing reaching the thigh. Nothing reaching at all. Within seconds of the boys walking through the gate onto the poolside area they were met by lifeguards making the universal French sign of approbation: the pointer finger waving side to side to side to side while the finger-owner repeats slowly "no no no." Only bathing suits allowed, they were told. And bathing suits, they were further told, were what every other guy was wearing, the barest, in the full meaning of the word, minimum.

Dejected, rejected and objected, we walked to the office to tell our tale and see if we could get our money back. But the folks in the office had a solution. They took us by the hand and led us to the locker room. There was the dispensing machine. Between rows of Mars bars, Snickers and chewing gum were tiny packages containing bathing suits, Speedos in sizes small, tiny and infinitesimal.

The guys shivered for a moment, sucked up their courage and baggy lacrosse-wear was replaced with napkin-sized black bathing suits. It took a slide or two down the water slide before they forgot what they were wearing and spent the next few hours splashing away, looking decidedly

French, long lacrosse locks flowing even in the absence of a thread of lacrosse wear.

France won that battle in the culture wars. And two young Americans learned that not all the world is like Dover, New Hampshire. And there's nothing wrong with that.

Six months in France

We reached the six-month point in our initial two year French exodus. Some things became automatic: I don't attempt to stand up in the aft cabin, the former domicile of the family of Dutch dwarves who originally lived on HOOP DOET LEVEN, because I'd bump my head; Sandra hardly ever apologizes to the French for her French because they invariably reply that she speaks so well, or at least so much better than they speak English; chocolate croissants for breakfast every day are no longer a treat but are just what one has for breakfast, bien sur, and most of all, as did the world's most sympathetic woman in A Streetcar Named Desire, we came to rely on the kindness of strangers, French strangers.

Some things we miss. Family and friends, of course, but also bottomless cups of coffee, sitting at a table with friends for hour after hour as the waitress asks if we'd like just one more top-up and we nod, knowing we'll pay the price for a dozen cups of coffee later that day, and night. Here in France, of course, you also spend hour after hour at a cafe table, observing and being observed, but the coffee cup holds fewer drops than are normally slopped over the rim into the saucer at home, and there are no refills, or even reorders. Coffee is drunk as if it were rotgut whiskey at a cowboy saloon, one shot and then you are cut off. I have never, ever been asked if I wanted a second cup of coffee.

I used to miss the Simpsons until they showed up on our French TV in a hotel room, with Homer sounding sophisticated in French, Bart as suave as usual, Crusty the Clown so, well, so French.

Other things are just strange, so bizarre in fact, that they never become ordinary. The boat came with a combination DVD and videocassette player – player only, no recording – and a hundred or so DVDs and videocassettes, including what seems to be the complete filmography of Bruce Willis (except for that wonderful TV detective series he did with Cybil Shepherd, Moonlighting). The switch from videocassettes to DVDs must have happened about the time HOOP DOET LEVEN crossed the English Channel from London to France, as the cassettes have United Kingdom copyright warnings and the DVDs French ones. The movies on cassette are all in English; the DVDs, sometimes, will play in English with French subtitles, sometimes the reverse. The copyright warnings are cultural barometers. We know the familiar U.S. warning, blaring in all caps FBI WARNING YOU WILL BE LOCKED BEHIND BARS FOREVER AND BECOME THE SEX SLAVE OF OUTLAW BIKERS IF YOU COPY THIS MOVIE, as if the FBI has SWAT teams of crack agents busting down suburban doors to arrest five-year-olds watching bootleg copies of My Little Mermaid VIII. The British warning is oh so much more polite, reminding you that making, buying, watching or even holding in your hand unauthorized copies hurts people and just should not be done. The Brits add that the video is only for private use and commercial showing of this film is absolutely, totally, without question prohibited. Good enough and equally ineffective as siccing the FBI on you, but then the Brits get down to the details. Examples of locations at which this videocassette may not be played include, we are warned, "offshore oil platforms" and "prisons." Prisons? What did that British Film Board bureaucrat expect would happen, that the ax murderers, still-incarcerated Irish Republican Army bomb throwers, London Underground terrorists and Jack the Ripper rip offs herded into a darkened room atop the Tower of London, surrounded by truncheon-wielding prison guards, rattling their chains in a threatening rhythm demanding that Saving Nemo Part V start now, right this moment, that at the instant the warning about it being illegal to show this film in a prison appears on the screen the warden will smack his forehead in sudden appreciation of his incipient crime and yank the film projector plug from the socket? It is a tossup whether the U.S. FBI warning or the oh so polite British list of locations at which this film may not be shown demonstrates the greater estrangement from reality.

The French DVDs simply show two hands wringing in despair that Jerry Lewis and Bruce Willis never made a movie together, because what would be more sophisticated, more entertaining, more, well, more cultured?

Hardly a day passes when we don't ask each other where the stereotype of the rude French, the antipathy to all things French that pervades some parts and some people in the States came from. Is it simply a relic from the French government pointing out that neither did the emperor have any clothes nor did Saddam have any weapons of mass destruction when the United States was locked into "shock and awe" mode and we watched smart bombs fall on Baghdad live and in color, back in the days when Congress created "freedom fries" in retaliation for the French wiggling their pointer fingers and muttering "no, no, no" to the Gulf War Part Two?

People are just so nice to us. Here's an example. We were in Besançon, a medieval city dominated by a fortress on a precipice overlooking the city, backed by bastions along the river front and stone walls with firing slits at regular intervals, a fortress of a city, or a city within a fortress. This obsession with defense may be explained by the unfortunate Dark Ages sacking of the city by the Barbarians, not some generic horde of small B barbarians, but the capital B Barbarians themselves, the tribe all future barbarians were named after. Imagine how truly bad those original Barbarians must have been to have their name become generic for badness, as kleenex is for tissues and escalator is for, well, for escalators (the tribe of Vandals probably came a close second on the truly-bad scale). In one of those voila moments that strike when learning French, I suddenly connected the word "barbe," which means beard (and yet, of course, is a feminine noun), with the term "barbarian," as in, "bearded people." Neat, huh?

Besançon's original watch and clock industry has morphed into a biotech center churning out artificial hearts and micro-robotic probes. An altogether fascinating and charming city dominated by the River Doubs, which surrounds it on three sides. We, however, were faced with a more mundane task: restocking our pantry after two weeks of feeding two young men, our grandchildren, who when asked what they wanted for lunch replied "a lot." We needed a grocery store. The nearest one to where we were moored was several miles bike ride away. We loaded our panniers on the bikes and pedaled off through twisting medieval streets, up and down steep hills, alongside stone bastions with double levels of cannon slots. We eventually found the grocery, or at least a grocery if not the specific grocery we'd so carefully plotted a route to. We did our shopping, pondering whether to pick up the frozen escargot, finally deciding that the fresh were so much better. Leaving the store to return to the boat, I pointed right. Sandra pointed left. We rode straight into oblivion. Thirty minutes later I waived down another cyclist and used the latest addition to my French vocabulary, "pardon monsieur, je suis perdu," ("Excuse me kind stranger. I am so lost I rode out of New York this morning and I suspect I may be in France but beyond that I haven't a clue as to where I am. Take pity on me, please.") Follow me, the man replied, standing in his saddle, the first man ever to leave rubber on a bicycle. Not since Gene Hackman raced under the elevated tracks in The French Connection has such a Gallic chase taken place. Our guide pedaled frantically as I remained glued to his rear wheel and Sandra kept me in sight, up vertical cliffs, down mountain sides, face to face with buses, crossing lanes of traffic, round about roundabouts, until we chickened out at a red light, with the river, and the boat, almost in sight.

"We never got to thank him," Sandra muttered. We rode on after the light turned green and our hearts ceased their rock and roll rhythms. And there he was, waiting for us. He had not yet shaken our hands and wished us "bon vacances," a "good vacation" (the French wish each other a "bon" everything, "bon weekend," "bon promenade," and of course, "bon jour." When we bought the new water heater for the boat the woman who'd helped us select it wished us a "bon douche," a good shower). Then he shook our hands, thanking us for giving him the opportunity to be of assistance.

After experiences such as this, which happen nearly every day, we'll never call them freedom fries, but then, the French don't call them French fries, nor do they eat French toast or French vanilla ice cream.

Going where no barge can go

We took the Marne au Rhin Canal from Lorraine, in northern France, eastward to Alsace, on the German border. Friends were meeting us in Alsace and we had some extra time until they arrived. We decided to escape from the barge for a bit. Which led to the next adventure.

With some trepidation I surreptitiously checked out the guy standing on my right in the cable car taking us up into the clouds next to Mt. Blanc in the French Alps. He casually flipped his medieval-looking ice axe, spinning it in the air and catching it by the handle. A rock climbing helmet dangled from his belt. Hmm. I looked left. This guy had a coil of about a mile of multi-colored rope over his shoulder. On his back he wore a Hydration System. I know it was a Hydration System because it said so in bold orange letters. Plastic tubes ran over his shoulder from his Hydration System to a container strapped to his back. He could slurp Hydration Fluid – I knew it could not hold ordinary water – by turning his head. An assortment of twenty or so carabineers, which I thought were only used by cool kids to hold their key collections to their belt loops, dangled from his pack. His ice axe hung from a sling attached to his Hydration System. The man and woman in front of us lugged gigundo

122

red backpacks. With their parachutes – or more accurately, their paragliders – stuffed inside. They weren't planning on walking down.

Obviously, equipment was a big deal here. Nobody seemed especially impressed with the red LL Bean book bag on my back. It held an extra WoodenBoat Magazine tee shirt. And an apple. Sandra lugged her own apple. And half a bar of Toblerone. We'd topped up the orange juice carton with water that morning and I carried that in my book bag. It was our Hydration System. Tropicana, I think. I was the only one on the mountain with a backpack that had a separate compartment for a pencil sharpener. And an eraser. And a homework planner. We glanced at each other. And waited for the cable car to emerge from the clouds. Then, when it did, we hoped the clouds would return. It was a long way down and we were a long way up.

We were in Chamonix, in the French Alps, a long, long way, horizontally and vertically, from Hoop Doet Leven.

The barge was tied securely to the quay in Lutzelbourg, on the Lorraine-Alsace border. We took the train to Strasbourg, on the French-German border, spent a few days there, then rented a car and drove to Chamonix, in the French Alps. We'd rented a little cabin through AirBNB at the foot of Mt. Blanc, Europe's highest mountain.

Our goal was to get some time away from the boat to a place far from the canals. The Alps. It turned out the shortest distance from Strasbourg, in France, to Chamonix, in France, was to drive across Switzerland. Somebody had mentioned that "Switzerland is not in Europe" but I was pretty sure I'd seen it there on a map, pretty much dead center in Europe in fact. As it turned out, "Europe," to Europeans, is a political entity, not a geographic place. Switzerland, for reasons that probably make sense to the Swiss, being Swiss, is not a member of the European Union. That meant three things for us, pretty much at the moment we crossed the border. First, we had to stop at a border crossing, something we hadn't seen previously in present-day Europe. After all, we'd walked from France into Italy one afternoon – the coffee is better in Italy – and the former customs post was derelict. Then came the second surprise. But first a digression.

We live in Massachusetts, on the Northeast coast, the upper right hand corner of the States. Up the coast from us is New Hampshire. Just north of New Hampshire is Maine. Maine bills itself on billboards and, until recently, on its automobile license plates, as Vacationland. According to Maine's tourist office, 23 million people drive to the state for their summer vacations. Without stopping in New Hampshire. New Hampshire has its own in-your-face state motto of Live Free or Die. Says so on their license plates. Not surprisingly, New Hampshire has no state income tax. What New Hampshire does have is fourteen miles (about twenty-two kilometers) of coastline between Massachusetts to the south and Maine to the North. Strategically, the interstate highway from pretty much anywhere that isn't Canada to everywhere that is Maine Vacationland runs along that fourteen mile New Hampshire coast. So, rather than tax its own residents, the Live Free (at least Tax Free) or Die folks planted a toll booth across the highway and elicit a dollar from every carload of the 23 million vacationers whizzing north to Maine's Vacationland.

Which brings me to the second surprise on entering Switzerland. Since it is not part of "Europe," Switzerland doesn't receive any highway money from the European Union. Instead, a polite young woman speaking impeccable English stopped us at the border crossing and informed us that we would have to pay a Swiss road tax of 33 euros, about $45. We reluctantly handed her 40 euros in exchange for a red windshield sticker. She consoled us by saying it was good for a year. I replied that the car was rented for a week. She smiled and said, "I suppose you don't care where I stick it on the windshield then." And gave us change from the 40 euros. New Hampshire highway officials should be humbled by the Swiss.

Which led to the third surprise. Switzerland, not part of Europe, does not use euros. Our 7 euros change was delivered in Swiss francs, which we had about two hours to spend before we reentered France. And Europe. As it turned out, we had just enough Swiss francs to purchase two Toblerone bars at the next highway rest area. Thus the remaining Toblerone in Sandra's pack as we rode the cable car into the clouds.

We did three long hikes through the mountains. And exercised great discretion in choosing not to take a shortcut down from one mountain in a tandem paraglider. It might not be wisdom that comes with age. But it could be a somewhat reasonable facsimile thereof.

I survived our mountain hikes above Chamonix, aided by the purchase of a pair of batons, basically ski poles with no snow baskets on the ends, which helped shove me up hill and down. We had a snowball fight on July 1. And went out for fondue. And had dinner with an actual Chamonix mountain guide, who owned the cabin we rented, with his wife, who managed it. Chamonix has the oldest certified mountain guide service in the world. Its numbers are strictly limited. Qualification is rigorous and takes years. Our jaws dropped as we listened to his stories about climbing Kilimanjaro six times, climbing in the Andes, climbing in the Antarctic, climbing throughout the Himalayas – including Everest. We complained about the thin air we experienced on the Aiguile du Midi at 3,842 meters (12,605 feet) and asked at what height he used oxygen. He smiled. "I have never used oxygen," he said.

We returned to the barge, to Saverne, in Alsace. Back in thick air with lots of oxygen. But adventure lurked even there.

Our first night back was the World Cup elimination match between France and Germany. The World Cup is not a Big Thing in France. It is The Only Thing. Picture the World Series, the Super Bowl, the Stanley Cup and Mardi Gras rolled into one event. With a few thousand years of on and off animosity between the countries each team represents. Especially in Alsace, straddling the French-German border, in a region that flip-flopped between being part of Germany and part of France after each succeeding war, presently French but stuffed with German tourists.

This match was a Big Event. The Germans took over the main square in Saverne, waving flags, drinking beer, singing rousing - disturbingly rousing to be honest - songs. The French held their own. Picture the scene in "Casablanca" where the German officers in Rick's Cafe Americain gather around Sam's piano and sing "Die Wacht am Rhein" ("The Watch on the Rhine," a patriotic song intended to intimidate whatever country happens to be on the other side of the Rhine, i.e. France), Victor Lazlo then orders the band to play La Marseillaise. Rick nods approval and the French drown out the Germans. (Check the translation for the French national anthem: "The tyrants are coming into our midst to cut the throats of your sons and consorts." Consorts, apparently, take priority over wives and daughters. See, http://www.marseillaise.org/english/translation.html?standard).

Saverne felt like a night out at Rick's Cafe. We were cheering for the French but braced for the worst. A few nights earlier, when Germany beat Algeria, the local Algerians vented their displeasure by burning a car, though inexplicably not a German car. The scorch marks were right next to where we moored. Germans seem more restrained but a loss to France could have instigated an angry act of impoliteness, such as a visit from the Panzer Corps. But it was not to be. France lost 1-0. The town wallowed in pastis and the local beer, Licorne (which is exceptionally good, by the way, especially the Black wheat beer.)

We fought the law and we won, sort of

Hoop Doet Leven spent a month at the town mooring in Lutzelbourg, a picture book pretty town in Alsace, while we explored this semi-French, semi-German, mostly just plain Alsatian region and waited for our friends to arrive from Massachusetts. Lutzelbourg was the first town to the east of the mechanical marvel of the Arzviller Inclined Plane Boat Lift, a gigantic bathtub into which you motored your boat and were slowly slid up or down the side of a hill, duplicating a vertical journey in 15 minutes that used to take barges a full day through a series of locks. The Arzviller Lift was dramatic, thrilling, scenic, efficient.

When it worked.

The previous summer, the gates closed when a loaded passenger boat was half in and half out of the bathtub, jamming the works for the next ten months. But all was well. Arzviller was repaired and it reopened a month before our arrival. Lutzelbourg was the first town to the east of Arzviller.

The German side of the boat lift. Not the French side.

That was a distinction soon to assume significance.

In the mean time, however, we spent a few nights in Strasbourg, home of the European Parliament and a city that declares, on pretty much every vertical surface from the sides of buses and trams to half the city's billboards, that Strasbourg is The Europtimist. Oh, if only saying so could make it so. But it is a magnificent, historic city nonetheless. For a person such as myself for whom the most significant celebration of the year is the Annual Boston Science Fiction Marathon – a 24-hour orgy of viewing sci-fi films – even more important than the European Parliament is that Strasbourg is the home of the International Space University (www.isunet.edu), offering a Masters in Space Studies degree, among others. Courses are offered in English, French and Klingon.

Our friends arrived. We spent a few days canalling with them between Saverne and Lutzelbourg, a few days driving through Alsace in their rental car, and a night at a dairy farm high in the Vosges Mountains at which the fourth generation dairy farmer churns out kilograms of Munster cheese every day. We'd been anticipating his family-recipe Munster for weeks. We were surprised, which is a polite word for grossly disappointed, when at the farm dinner he served we went straight from the main course to the dessert. Where was the cheese course, we wondered. Sandra asked, politely, of course, if at a farm where the principle product was Munster cheese it was at all possible to have a cheese course, for which we would gladly pay whatever additional charge might be imposed. The farmer smiled in embarrassment and, moments later, delivered a platter of three monsters – young, middle-aged and elderly – and a brick of his own butter. He apologized. He'd never had American guests before. He did not think Americans ate smelly cheese. He was wrong. We ate everything. Including the butter brick. He brought a pie stuffed with that afternoon's Munster curds for dessert. Breakfast included more Munster.

The farm was nearly perfect. But we'd mistimed our visit. Two days later the Tour de France cycled right past. We didn't see the actual Tour de France – meaning guys riding bikes – but we walked the route past the farm in the Vosges Mountains and thought about collecting an official Tour de France trash bag.

Nonetheless, after five weeks in Alsace we were more than ready to do a demi tour – a 180-degree turnaround – and head the barge back to what we referred to simply as "France." Scoot up the Arzviller Lift, down the canal and we'd be in Lorraine, eating quiche instead of sauerkraut.

Alsace was nice, good wine and lots of it, nice cheeses. Heavy food. Interesting history. But enough was enough. It was time to go "home" to Bourgogne, Burgundy.

But we'd forgotten that most basic of French phrases.

Non, non, non.

Recall how the Arzviller Lift broke down the previous summer. Recall how they spent 1.6 million euros and ten months repairing the Lift, the tracks, the cables, the supports, the gears, the gates, the moving tub. Pretty much everything that moved was repaired or replaced. Pretty much everything. But not the wheels. Which fell off. Two days before we were due to ride up the Lift and back to France. VNF – the Voies Navigable de France, the waterways authority – announced Arzviller would be shut down for three days. Then three weeks. Then three months. The present target date for reopening was July.

Next July.

We were trapped, trapped between a broken boat lift that blocked the only water route back to France to the west, and Germany, to the east. We had about 15 kilometers – nine miles – of canal in which to cruise. Back and forth. Forth and back. Until the next July. Maybe.

Ah, but all was not lost. There was a way out. Sort of. Right smack between France and Germany is the Rhine River, the largest river in western Europe. If we went south on the Rhine, against the current, for 72 kilometers we'd come out at the French city of Mulhouse (rhymes with Toulouse - "too loose" - figure that one out). We'd been on some big rivers already, the Seine, the Saone, the Yonne. Big currents. Big ships. Big locks. But no big deal.

But those were big French rivers. The Rhine, being half French and half German was managed by the Rhine River Authority, an international body that operates independently from French and German regulations. We had to comply with the official Rhine Regulations, a set of rules created partly by the French and partly by the Germans. Most likely, the French contribution was the accordion playing in the background while the Germans dreamed up licensing schemes, inspection standards, rights of way regulations, and designs for the rubber stamps that must be slammed on each document before a boat can possibly float on the sacred Rhine.

It turned out that our barge absolutely had to have a Rhine certification before it would be allowed through the lock from the French canal onto the international Rhine. The boat already has a six-page safety certification, written in Dutch, good for pretty much every canal, stream, river and lake west of the Ural Mountains. But not the Rhine. We would have to weld two steel bulkheads isolating the engine compartment, for starters. That wasn't going to happen.

Fortunately, while the Germans were in charge of the regulations, the French were responsible for the exceptions. A few hours at the Strasbourg VNF office and we had in hand an official one-time-only permit good until the end of August to take Hoop Doet Leven on the Rhine, duly stamped, embossed and executed by Le Chef himself, all in French. Voila, we thought.

Not quite voila, it turned out.

Besides the boat needing a Rhine license, so did le Captaine. While we're both licensed by the European waterways consortium to operate Hoop Doet Leven on pretty much every drop of European waters, that license isn't good enough for the Rhine. My American commercial license, which permits me to carry an unlimited number of paying passengers on any boat up to 50 tons up to 200 miles offshore through hurricanes and fog, past rocky shores and crowded harbors, similarly would not open the door to the Rhine. And besides, I hadn't had a Rhine medical examination proving I had the physical, mental and emotional toughness to captain my barge on that river. I could get a medical certificate, I was told. In Switzerland.

The boat could travel on the Rhine. But we couldn't. This was frustrating, to say the least.

The only remaining option, we were told, was to hire an Official Rhine Pilot to guide our barge up the river for a couple of days. At 250 euros a day. Now there might have been some justification for all this regulation if the body of water we were considering navigating was some raging torrent with whirlpools, sandbanks, random rocks. Sharks. German U-boats. But the Rhine from just south of Strasbourg to just east of Mulhouse, the 72 kilometers we wanted to travel to get back to France, is more a canal than a river. It isn't even called the Rhine, but is officially called the Grand Canal d' Alsace. The river banks are sloping concrete. Every ten kilometers or so a dam crosses the river, slowing and controlling the current, and generating electricity. At every dam is a wide lock that lifts boats up or down. Basically all you do, all you can possibly do, on this stretch of Rhine, is drive straight ahead when the river is straight, drive around a curve when it curves, wait for the lock doors to open and drive your boat in to a lock that is the size of a football field. It isn't all that difficult. It staggers the imagination to come up with what the certified, licensed, Official Rhine Pilot would have done for two days except say to go straight when the river was straight and to turn when the river turned.

But we did try to find a Rhine pilot. They aren't listed in the telephone book. They aren't even listed on the internet. The Strasbourg Port Authority had no idea what we were talking about when we asked to hire a pilot. Finally, in desperation, we followed the only advice we received from VNF about how to find an Official Rhine Pilot. I stood at a canal lock next to our mooring in the town of Soufellweyersheim – see why we were desperate to get back to the French part of France – where two commercial barges passed each day traveling to and from a cement plant, and when they stopped at the lock I asked the captains if they knew of any Rhine pilots. They did. Good. They wrote down their names and telephone numbers. Better. We, meaning Sandra, called and was told that, yes, I am a Rhine pilot and I will call you back when I can take your boat. Fantastic.

We're still waiting for the call back. Bummer. It is summer and that is when Rhine pilots, being French, are on vacation. Perhaps we could go in February.

Well, enough was enough. We were Bonnie and Clyde. Butch Cassidy and the Sundance Kid. Damn the torpedoes, full speed ahead. We would just go. What's the worst that could happen?

The German Wasserpolice, that's the worst that could happen. Fast, gray boats stuffed with men aching to utter those words that sent icicles into the hearts of American spies in World War II movies. Show me your papers. Wasserpolice prison.

Our solution? We slipped onto the Rhine on a Saturday morning and continued at dawn on a rainy Sunday, with thunder clashing and lightening flashing, confident that the Wasserpolice were tucked under their eiderdowns sleeping off Friday and Saturday nights' schnapps and schnitzel. And it worked. Although we were surrounded by commercial barges that barely squeezed into the locks, ships that were wider than we were long, the biggest problem we faced for two days was the current running against us at six kilometers an hour.

We burned through a lot of fuel and ran our engine higher than we'd ever run it. But neither the giant river squids we probably would have learned about had we attended Rhine Pilot University nor the dreaded Wasserpolice captured us.

We escaped from the Rhine at the Niffer lock near Mulhouse unscathed and unincarcerated. We puttered onto a canal on Sunday afternoon. And celebrated. We headed west on the Rhone au Rhin Canal at sedate canal speeds, through fields and villages. Downhill. Down the River Doubs. Toward the River Saone. Toward Bourgogne. Toward the French part of France.

A cheesey experience

The River Doubs (pronounced "dew" – has anybody French ever pondered whether there is any redeeming social value in having a language in which almost half of the letters in any word do nothing but take up space) arises in the Jura Massif near the Swiss border. Eventually, it becomes an on-again, off-again portion of the Canal du Rhone au Rhin(e) (The name of the river we'd just left has a final "e" in German and English but not in French, which doesn't much matter since the French wouldn't pronounce it anyway). The canal connects the Rhine River in the east, on the German border, with the Saone and the Rhone Rivers, running north and south through the center of France, down to the Mediterranean at Marseilles. It's a beautiful river, with steep gorges on both sides.

Beautiful except when it rains. And the river rises. And gentle barging becomes white water rafting. Then the waterways authority, with eminent good sense, slams shuts the steel doors on the various portes de garde – guard doors that shut off the roaring river sections from the placid canal sections – and navigation comes to a halt.

That is what happened after we left the Rhine and escaped to the French part of France. We were at Montbeliard (don't pronounce the "t" or the "d," or you know what, just go ahead and do it; they won't care), the namesake for brown and white Montbeliard cows (think chocolate Holsteins) and the saucisse de Montbeliard, the Montbeliard sausage, which is entirely porcine and is not made at all from Montbeliard cows but, nonetheless, is the champagne of sausages, the ultimate hot dog. Montbeliard is also the home of the automaker (and bicycle maker) Peugeot. Think French Detroit. But with better food and wine. And no bankruptcy.

We took the canal closing as an opportunity to see what was over the hills and not too far away. We rented a car from our usual rental company – Europcar – booking it through our usual rental car booking company – AutoEurope, located in Portland, Maine, not all that far from our home north of Boston. For some reason we get better prices going through the U.S. agency, using a U.S. credit card, than by going directly to the French company with a French bank card. The Montbeliard Europecar agency is located literally at the front door of the massive Peugeot factory that occupies a significant percentage of the landscape around the city. Peugeots are nice cars. We looked forward to renting one. However, excited to have American customers, the rental company bestowed upon us a Ford. As a favor. When we asked they said they didn't have a Peugeot available. Right. Go across the street and knock on the front door. To show we were not disappointed Sandra explained that she grew up in Dearborn, Michigan, the home of Ford. Dearborn, the Montbeliard of the U.S.

Driving in France is not all that difficult, not at all . . . except for the dreaded priorite a droite, the priority of the right law. There was a time, not all that long ago, when a wagon filled with hay drawn by a hot, tired horse rolled slowly toward a cross-road. At the same time a wood gatherer returning from gathering wood in the forest led his donkey, loaded with fallen branches, toward the same cross-road. Pierre, with the donkey, would see Jean Claude, with the horse and wagon, approaching on his right. They would waive at one another. Comment on the hot weather. Arrange to meet later for a pastis at the bar. Then Jean Claude, being on

the right, went through the intersection first, wav'
long friend. That is priorite a droite. The vehicle
tions has right of way. Fast forward to our dep
As we drove, slowly, through towns and vill
from every narrow lane and way, at least ev
out shot Peugeots, Renaults and Citroens ?
they turned left or right, eyes straight forward, cu.
BEING ON THE RIGHT, they had priority. This ..
road is supposedly being phased out. Supposedly, we say, ʋ
are no signs indicating where it is in effect and where it isn't. Anʋ
you stop to allow the car on your right to proceed, the driver behind yoʋ
will immediately let you know that this is an intersection where everybody
knows that such a silly old law was abandoned years ago. The driver on
your right, being of the old school, will naturally take advantage of your
ignorance and shoot in front of you. Seeing that, Madame, who is driving
three inches from your rear fender, is stunned by your ignorance and
jams both elbows on her horn as a gentle lesson for you.

Otherwise, driving is no problem.

Except for road signs. Most signs are fairly self explanatory. We still
haven't figured out direction signs giving the name of a town and an arrow, which the French place at precisely 45 degrees at intersections exactly splitting the difference between the roads to right and left, leaving
you to wonder which road the sign is telling you to follow. But even in
English-phobic France, signs say "Stop" rather than "Arrêter." Parking is
indicated with a large "P" even though the word for parking is "stationnement" (although signs that tell you "no parking" say "stationnement
interdit;" France can yield to Englishification just so much).

We drove up into the Jura Mountains on the first weekend of
August, joining the rest of France on vacation. Living wild and free, we'd
made no reservations and had little idea where we would stay for the four
nights we hoped it would take for the river to settle down. Our main goal
was to learn about, purchase and consume Comte (pronounced "con-
tay," because it is more interesting if the "m" sounds like an "n," just this
once) cheese made in the Jura, among our favorite French cheeses.

We arrived at Salins les Bains, a town named for its salt, recently
made a UNESCO World Heritage Site for the historic salt works there.
The first stop was the museum of salt. (France has a "museum of . . ."
just about everything; somewhere there must be a Museum of Museums).

d to the underground vaults where over the centuries wells
ug to deep deposits of salt water. This water was pumped to
e and run into copper trays. Fires were built under the trays to
te the water and salt was shoveled out. Tons and tons and tons of
r hundreds and hundreds of years, a goodly portion of France's salt.
ay, salt comes from other sources. The town uses the salty water to
elt snow on its streets in the winter.

Interesting for sure. But it wasn't cheese. The hunt continued.

We went to the tourist information office in Salins les Bains and explained that we wanted to stay at a farm. Where they made Comte. The
woman thought for a while and said there might be a place. She made a
phone call and said, yes, they had a room. Did we want to drive to the
farm and see it? Certainly, we replied.

Thus we found la Grange Combaret (www.grange-combaret.com).
What had been the farm's barn until it burned down a few years ago was
rebuilt as an auberge, a country inn with four guest rooms and a long dining table. Our second floor room was a shock, huge, new, bright and with
a balcony overlooking the rest of the farm. And the herd of 40 Montbeliard milk cows. Sandra was in bovine heaven and made a beeline for the
dairy barn, toward which the cows were ambling for their afternoon milking, cow bells tinkling as they strolled down from the pasture. The
farmer, Denis, and his son Xavier were milking. Sandra told them that
her grandfather had been a dairy farmer.

All the farm's milk goes to the nearby cooperative fruitière (why a
cheesemaking operation is called a "fruitière" remains a mystery) where it
is made into 50 kilogram (110 pound) wheels of Comte cheese. Each
wheel requires 600 liters (160 gallons) of unpasteurized milk – about 30
cows' daily production. Because Comte production requires so much
milk, each town's farmers pool their production at the fruitière. After a
few weeks, the Comte wheels are shipped to the cave de affinage – the
aging facility – where the cheese is stored on old pine shelves for anywhere from a few months to several years, where it is regularly rubbed
with salt and turned over and over. All this fondling makes Comte special, we were told.

Does eating a two-year-old unpasteurized milk product worry you?
Try it, you'll like it.

Comte is a hard cheese, much like Gruyere, which is made just over
the border in the Swiss town of Gruyere – what an amazing coincidence.

The designation Comte is protected, an A.O.C. – Appelation de Origine Controlle – just like champagne that can only come from Champagne, or Montbeliard sausages that can only come from around Montbeliard. Comte has been made this way for centuries and still must be made under strict A.O.C. rules. For example, all the milk must come from Montbeliard cows. Each cow must have at least one hectare (about 2.5 acres) to graze. The cows must graze in the pastures and not be fed hay, except during the coldest winter months when they eat hay made from their regular pasture and the cheese is white rather than the yellow of summer cheese. The high mountain pastures contain 150 or so different grasses and wildflowers that impart rich flavors to the milk. The pastures can only be fertilized with compost produced on the farm with no chemicals. There's probably a regulation about the size of the cow bells. And maybe the farmer has to milk his cows left handed.

Each fruitière, where the milk is turned into cheese, is owned cooperatively by the local farmers since the Comte standard allows milk to be transported no more than 14 kilometers from farm to fruitière. As a result, each fruitière's Comte reflects – to use the untranslatable French word that extols most everything local – the terroir of the local pastures. Just as wine from one town in Bourgogne – Burgundy – is distinctively different from wine made from identical grapes in the next town, so Comte cheese made at one fruitièrie is different from the next town's cheese. Different because milk from different pastures with different blends of grasses and flowers has different flavors. Different because the cheesemaker is different. Different because, being France, each town makes the best Comte. Just ask anybody in the town.

And different because the affinage – the aging process – is different. During affinage hundreds of rounds of cheese are tucked away in caves, stone sheds and special aging vaults. As their time of readiness approaches, the affinage expert – the affineur – goes from wheel to wheel tapping the top of the wheel with a small hammer called a sonde, listening for the sounds. They hear distinctions ordinary mortals don't hear. (Bringing to mind the time we accompanied Sandra's father, a professional drummer, to a drum shop in Nashville, Tennessee to shop for a new cymbal. He spent an hour in the shop's cymbal room, tapping each of the hundreds of cymbals on display. At the end he didn't buy anything. They didn't have one with the sound he was looking for, he said). The cheese tells you when it is ready to eat. At least it tells the affineur.

Now this seems like an awful lot of effort for something as straight-forward as a piece of cheese. After all, we come from a place where most of what is sold as "cheese" is required by law to include the word "prod-uct," as in "cheese product," on the label, to distinguish it from a food item that is made entirely from, what shall we say, milk rather than what could be a petrochemical. American cheese technology progressed from the solid brick of cheese to the wonder of presliced cheese to the ultimate luxury of individually wrapped-in-plastic slices of cheese. Flavor has never been a priority when it comes to the cheese product called Ameri-can cheese. Uniform meltworthiness is a good thing. And texture, which has to be somewhat stretchy.

So Comte was a revelation to us.

We had dinner at the farm one night, chicken raised at the farm drenched in a sauce of, what else, Comte. Think chicken fondue. Think local, as in whatever we ate originated within sight of the kitchen window.

Our four-day cheese expedition was a success. We knew we liked Comte. Now we knew why. Like so much of France, what made it special was a blend of tradition, of expertise, of over the top attention to doing things right. And an added dose of magic.

We returned to the barge. The river settled down and we raced to the end of the canal before the next set of rain storms arrived. We safely set-tled back in the France we know best, Bourgogne, tied to the stone wall in the port at Dijon for a few weeks. We could buy Comte at the fromagerie in Dijon, but our first night's cheese was stinky Epoisse de Bourgogne, described as a pungent unpasteurized cows milk, smear-ripened (meaning it is rinsed in a local liquor) orange cheese made a short ways up the Canal du Bourgogne. At a town called Epoisse. It was Napo-leon's favorite cheese.

That is how France works.

Plan B for winter

With the departure of our grandchildren and the end of summer, we turned the barge toward our planned winter home of Epinal, a city in the Vosges, a hilly region in northeastern France. By mid-September the nights turned chilly. No, the nights turned downright cold and the winter-weight down comforter was dragged out from its storage bag (a gigundo version of a ziplock sandwich bag with a valve that hooks to the vacuum cleaner, a set of twelve of which I had tucked away, along with eight magic Ginzu knives – "cuts steel and slices paper!" – my Popeil Pocket Fisherman -"fits in your glove compartment for all those times you have to fish RIGHT NOW" – and my Bassomatic juicer; some people can't resist making a toll-free call at 3:00 a.m. after a 45 minute infomercial between science fiction films. You've wondered who buys all that junk in infomercials. C'est moi. Its me).

It was getting to be time to think about the Other Half of the year in France, the six months during which the barge would stay in one place and we would travel through Europe the way normal people do, by train and plane.

We set off on our mission to Epinal, 250 kilometers and 90 locks away from Dijon. Epinal has a wide mooring basin with stone walls and electricity and water available all winter. We'd traveled there in our rental car shortly after we'd first arrived in France and loved the city. We played it safe, or so we thought, and reserved a winter mooring space, paying a deposit of 200 euros to hold our spot. Oh how clever and cautious we were. Most of the trip would be up the River Saone, wide, deep and slow-moving so late in the year, with widely-spaced locks, perfect for covering many kilometers each day. All in all, easy smug barging.

But, as we hear every day in France, somebody tells somebody, with thumb outstretched and pointer finger waving from side to side, "no, no, no."

We were not to go to Epinal. "No, no, no."

Epinal is located on an old canal that seems to change its name from time to time. Our charts – which admittedly were printed in 1991, but, then, canals and rivers move their positions awfully slowly – called the canal the Canal de l'Est (sud branch). Other maps called it the Canal de Vosges. Under whatever name, we learned that Epinal is not quite "on" the canal, but is pretty "near" it. It turns out the difference between being "on" and "near" is significant, as in the difference between "winter in Epinal" and, as the apocryphal story about asking directions in Maine goes, "ya cain't get thee-ya from hee-ya." What connects the harbor in Epinal with the nearby canal is a three kilometer long "deviation," a small canal with no locks, but a flooded nautical bridge that takes boats over a river. That three kilometer canal is shallow. In summers such as this one, which got off to a wet start but turned dry, "shallow" became that Maine expression.

According to the canal authority web site, we just couldn't get there, or more precisely, we could but the barge, which needs 1.3 meters of water to float in, couldn't. We were in the same situation as a radio conversation I'd overheard in Florida on the Intracoastal Waterway, in which a self-important sounding skipper called a bridge tender on the radio demanding to know if he needed the bridge to open for him and saying his boat required a clearance of twenty feet. Will my boat fit under the bridge, he shouted into his radio. The bridge tender calmly replied, "most of it will." Well, most of HOOP DOET LEVEN could get through the Epinal canal, but certainly not the lower few feet of the boat, not without lowering our wheels.

This seemed an odd situation. We called the harbormaster – the Port Capitaine – in Epinal. He spoke no English but understood Sandra's increasingly coherent French. He seemed to tell us just to come, not to worry, see you soon, thanks for calling, and some other things, none of which included that the port and the canal had shut down for the winter, that every boat in the port had to leave by the middle of August and that he was a Capitaine de port without a port to be Capitaine of. Nonetheless, that telephone conversation encouraged us to head north, up the river toward Epinal. Sandra was less confident in her French comprehension, however, and we asked the daughter of some Ipswich friends, a daughter living in France and speaking French, if she would telephone the canal authority – VNF – for us and confirm that we would be able to float all the way to Epinal. She made the call and reported back that VNF said the canal to Epinal was closed for the winter. Closed as in there is a metal chain from one bank to the other that won't be unlocked until March, or maybe April. Go someplace else, they said. Anyplace but not Epinal.

Before Sandra clicked off the cell phone I had the boat doing an abrupt U-turn in the middle of the River Saone. It was time for Plan B for winter.

Fortunately, we were not far from Saint Jean de Losne ("the Barge Capital of France"). We found winter space at a recently-constructed facility in the nearby town of Auxonne. This would put us in Bourgogne so there would be snails all winter and wine, wine and more wine. It is a 30 minute train ride to Dijon, so we would never run out of mustard, and Sandra could take French lessons there.

We were fortuitously struck by serendipity once again.

American politics, from afar

As we settled into our winter home in Auxonne the U.S. presidential election settled into its final weeks, Obama or Romney. We followed closely, although from afar and through our own jaundiced eyes. Sandra read La Monde, a slightly left-leaning Paris newspaper, online every morning. I absorbed the New York Times on my iPad every morning, in fact, pretty much every morning since junior high school. The Times - and a gargantuan collection of science fiction books - shaped my view of the world. The barge was entirely Fox free.

Our main source of up-to-the-instant news, as with most everybody else in France, was from posters displayed on the sidewalk in front of neighborhood tabacs, the   ubiquitous news/cigarette/candy/gossip stores that alternate with dog grooming salons, driving schools and hairdressers for French sidewalk commerce. Newspapers distribute these posters with each edition. The sidewalk in front of the tabac is blockaded with posters shouting the most important events of the day in lurid capital letters. It was from a poster in front of a tabac that I learned, for example, that Celine Dion was expecting Prince William's love child, that Carla Bruni was "liberated" from Nicholas Sarkozy when he lost the election, and that Michelle Obama has the best arms in America.

A tabac poster summed up the French perspective on the American presidential race:

"Mitt Romney, extraterrestre?" it inquired in six-inch high letters, accompanied by a far from flattering photo.

Extraterrestrial. As in E.T. phone home. Besides summarizing the French view of the Republican candidate for Leader of the Free World, the question raised the issue of illegal aliens to a new level.

American politics are a puzzle here. To some French, America seems to be as dominated as is Iran by medieval-thinking religious zealots. They read that a majority of Americans believe in neither global warming nor evolution. They ask, in all seriousness, if Americans really think their president is a Muslim. French newspapers report each mass shooting as if Wyatt Earp is still hunting down Billy the Kid and the Younger Gang in downtown Denver, as if Dirty Harry, NYPD, 24, CSI, and probably Dragnet and the Mod Squad accurately represent everyday life in America. After all, France is a country in which we could go for an entire week without hearing anybody, man, woman, child or even dog, raise their voice. They simply cannot fathom reading about Americans demanding, and receiving, the right to carry concealed automatics to university classes, in handbags, in their cars. The closest we came to being the victims of crime was the night when three young men, who'd obviously had a tad too much Bordeaux, climbed onto the boat at 3:00 a.m. and took cellphone photos of each other. The concept of a Sunday promenade through Dijon packing a .38 revolver is simply, well, simply foreign. The French were incensed about losing the right to have cigarettes in bars, but they easily understand that perhaps Pernod and pistols are not a safe mixture.

We went to the movies in Dijon. Saw Oliver Stone's "Savages," about a pair of surfer pot growers in Southern California who are confronted by a Mexican drug cartel. (We were not at all influenced by the fact that the film starred Taylor Kitsch, "Tim Riggins" of Friday Night Lights, which, with West Wing, filled our winter nights.) The America portrayed in this movie – sun-drenched California beaches studded with houses perching on cliffs, exotic cars pegging their speedometers, shotguns, rifles and machine guns in every trunk – is consistent with both the ubiquitous American television shows and French newspaper headlines about crime in the U.S.. It was convincing enough fantasy to make us homesick. Almost.

America looms large in France. Just as Hagen Daz is merely a concocted pseudo-Danish-sounding trade name for American-made ice cream, just as IKEA seems to name its products by pulling letters blindly from a Swedish Scrabble board, young men and women throughout France wear tee shirts plastered with a hodge podge of American-sounding words, grafted together in combinations that are as incomprehensible to Americans as they are sophisticated to the French. "Official CIA Athletic Department," declared one shirt in Besançon. "NYPD Staff," said a sweatshirt in Dole. Franklin & Marshall College, a relatively obscure Pennsylvania school, appears to have sold, or had stolen, its marketing rights. "Franklin & Marshall" tee shirts, sweat shirts, backpacks, are a hundred times more common than any American college anybody has heard of. Even American city names are sprinkled at random for equally random purposes. As acts of loyalty to our City on the Hill, I ordered a few "Boston pizzas" and received totally inconsistent concoctions that bear not the slightest relation to anything Massachusettsian: pineapple, jambon (smoked ham slices) and creme fraiche. Even escargot. No baked beans.

So, grafted on top of this skewed conception of America as a mélange of religious nuts who believe dinosaurs roamed the Garden of Eden with Adam and Eve, gun-packing grandmothers, mass murderers blazing away on a daily basis, hot cars and sunny beaches, all protected by CIA agents stalking Islamic suicide bombers and special forces teams helicoptering onto rooftops, the French also received their own myopic view of the American presidential election. At a time the United States, Europe and the world are on financial pins and needles, when worldwide unemployment was at a crisis, when entire nations threatened to go bankrupt, the French didn't comprehend why American voters, yet again, were obsessed with abortion, gay marriage and guns. The two candidates themselves were a mystery. How did a country viewed as controlled by archconservative born again evangelical zealots – probably racists or the off-spring of racists – end up with a black man running against a Mormon? And who is this Romney, they wondered. Remember, Romney's experience with France, the only experience of which the French are aware, was the 30 months he spent trying to convert them to an obscure American cult that believed American Indians were the lost tribes of Israel.

The French tolerate, perhaps even expect, some odd conduct by their politicians – mistresses, mistresses of mistresses, out-of-wedlock children, even somewhat fluid relations with the Germans – but kookiness is not a favored characteristic.

There are limits to how far the French would go. A presidential candidate descended from a polygamous cult that believes an angel revealed hidden golden tablets under a New York hill, just two years after the death of Napoleon, has no place on the spectrum of acceptable French politicians.

Perhaps, though, this is more a weakness of the French than a peculiarity of the United States. Despite American gunplay and playing with guns, despite the broad American distrust of science, the rejection, to be blunt, of reality, isn't it something to be proud of that little more than a hundred years ago, neither Obama nor Romney could have been conceived of as anything more than a bizarre aberration as a presidential candidate. This is a strength of America, and, perhaps, a limitation on the breadth of French politics.

So election night I went to bed early and woke at 2:00 a.m. Wednesday – 8:00 p.m. Eastern time Tuesday – and switched on the TV. Sandra had consented to swing the satellite dish from the French to the British satellite just for Election Day (Europe has free satellite reception since television is as much a universal human entitlement as is health care, and like health care, should be free, right?)

I switched between BBC News and France 24, an English language channel broadcast from France. And, I'll confess, after a few hours I also watched ABC and CBS news on the internet. The contrasts among the British, French and U.S. coverage of what was essentially the same event – endless analysis of the results of 3 percent of the returns from Nebraska – was fascinating. BBC, a disappointment, appeared to be doing its best to become the unacknowledged offspring of a clandestine mating between CNN and ABC/NBC/CBS nightly news. Lots of makeup, lots of hair, lots of flashing lights and computer animations. Worst of all was the rotating cast of guest commentators in matched American pairs of Democrat and Republican offering two heavily slanted interpretations on the mistaken assumption – the rule of thumb in U.S. news coverage – that two opinionated viewpoints will average out to reality. The broadcast was chaired and managed by Brits but most of the commentators were American. They seemed more interested in playing with their computer displays than in any substantive discussions.

French election coverage was quintessentially French. The men had carefully halted shaving three days before the broadcast. Steve Jobs model black mock turtlenecks and mock serious, mock snide expressions. The women lacked the heavy makeup, hair spray and poofing of the women on BBC, who were truly CNN-esque. Most of the commentators on the French broadcast were French journalists from magazines and websites. They offered their own analyses. Sometimes we agreed with them. Sometimes not. But they presented a contrast with the "balanced must mean fair" methodology of the BBC, and the U.S. networks.

Both French television and the BBC had teams of their own correspondents reporting from throughout the U.S., although their locations seemed odd, particularly when the BBC host segued into "and now here is Alistair reporting from the Peppermint Lounge in Las Vegas. He's got a nice gig tonight." Alistair then proceeded to interview the Nevada Republican chairman, who appeared to be spending election night perched on a stool at the bar, quite understandably firing down repeated glasses of scotch on the rocks with barely a pause.

It was a long night with long interludes between anything of any significance. Both the British and French broadcasts filled the gaps with discussions that would not have entertained a U.S. audience. BBC spent ten minutes on a discussion of why the Republicans are "Red" when they are not communists and the Democrats are "Blue" when they are not, whatever, Smurfs perhaps. An equal amount of time was spent on the French broadcast with a roundtable discussion of the question "is there anybody in France who supports Romney." The conclusion was that maybe a few French billionaires were Romney fans, but most of them moved out of the country when Francois Hollande announced he was raising income tax rates to 75 percent for them.

By the end, which for us came just as the sun was rising, I'd switched to Peter Jennings and ABC News. It was an American night.

On the next morning's baguette and pain au chocolate run I reminded my friendly boulangére (by that point in the winter I had spent so much time at the boulangerie that one of Sandra's French friends took her aside to inquire whether I might be having an affair with the baker's wife) that "Je suis un Américain" (I am an American) and that "Je suis très heureux aujourd'hui" (I am very happy today).

She smiled, replied "Obama est magnifique" and tossed in a free pain au chocolate as a sign of Franco-American comity.

Ah, but that election pales in comparison with next summer. Need I mention Bernie Sanders? The French would not be put off in the slightest by the concept of a Socialist running for high office. After all, they recently elected one. Hillary? Well, they did put an end to royalty in a revolution a few hundred years ago. Ted Cruz? Difficult to understand, perhaps.

Donald Trump? Merde.

I love Auxonne in the winter, when it drizzles

Winter. The view out the barge windows was the same, day after day. After day. After day. All summer I'd look out a window and had to think, "Now, where are we today?" We were mobile, every day a different place, a different adventure. For the winter, we might as well have been living in a house. Fixed in one place. The view never changed.

Well, that isn't quite right. Some mornings the view was of nothing at all. It seems we moored at Ground Zero of the French region of winter fogs. We shared the same vista as our friends living on Penobscot Bay in Maine – a landscape composed of the inside of a cloud. But the fog always cleared by lunch. Sometimes revealing sunshine. More often revealing higher clouds. Sometimes accompanied by rain. Actually, more often than not accompanied by rain. And wind. And chill. It does sound like Maine.

We settled into our routines. Sandra was booked every day: Monday mornings she taught English at the town's community center; Monday evenings she took French there; Tuesday she rode the train to Dijon for French lessons and lunches and coffee with her French online pen pals;

148

Wednesday we had an afternoon get-together with half a dozen English and French speakers to practice mutual language skills; Thursday was a get-together with a French couple on a neighboring boat to work on language; Fridays, Saturdays and Sundays were social occasions with other bargees, or dinners with French friends.

Our Auxonne social life was more full than winter life at home had been.

Thanksgiving away from family was difficult. We invited a French family – Sandra's tutor's – for dinner. Mom, dad, son and daughter. A night of food, wine, politics and trading "how we met" stories. And cultural revelations, such as failing to come up with an explanation for why Americans seem compelled to label so many "heroes:" every soldier, policeman, firefighter. The differences between America promoting "charity" to help distressed people while France sees helping people as part of the social compact for which government is created. And the revelation that an elementary school field trip went to a fromagerie – a cheese shop – so the children could learn how to select cheeses and the best methods to sample them. Has any American school ever included gastronomy as part of its elementary curriculum?

We developed routines. Friday was market day. Most winter Fridays, we bought a roasted chicken from the poulet roti man, a friendly fellow who parked his truck between the church and the Napoleon statue every Friday morning. He'd lift the side panel to reveal rows of chickens, ducks, quail and an assortment of most bird watchers' life lists slowly revolving in front of heating coils, the juice from the upper ones dripping onto the lower ones, and down to the potatoes at the bottom. He sold a soft sourdough bread in meter-long loafs; you spread your hands to show how much bread you wanted and paid by weight. Once you reached the head of the line, buying a chicken and chunk of bread took ten minutes of chatting. One week he offered to sharpen Sandra's kitchen knives. Another week he had to tell every customer behind us that when he asked if we wanted potatoes, I said oui and Sandra said no. Nobody complained about how slowly the line moved, instead they laughed along with us as each customer reached his turn to be the entertainment.

Another week, when I stood in line alone, when my turn arrived I pointed at the chicken I wanted, saying "celui-là," that one. No, no, no, the poulet roti man said, waving his finger of negativity from side to side at me. Madame would take that one, he instructed me, pointing at a different bird. I agreed to take the one madame would buy. He told everybody in line that I pointed to one bird but madame would want a different one and I wisely bought the bird madame wanted. They all laughed.

Not quite like getting your groceries scanned at the Stop-N-Shop.

So, we settled into our town of Auxonne, making friends, local and nautical, and learning our way through the intricacies of shopping, cooking, transportation and even health care. The French health care system is fantastic, and inexpensive, compared with the U.S., but it does hold its mysteries. For example, we wondered how to arrange for annual flu shots. At home we'd simply call our doctors' offices and schedule a time to get stuck. What to do here, we wondered? Tres facile, we were told. Just walk into a pharmacy, which are as ubiquitous as dog groomers, driving schools and boulangeries, and buy the vaccine. And it was tres simple, as we'd been told. Six euros later we held two fully-loaded syringes. Now what? A bit of Google on "how to inject flu vaccine" and there we sat in the barge, needles at hand, pants rolled down, courage evaporating. San-

dra bit the bullet and stuck herself, then she turned to me. I nodded bleakly and then, voila, she jabbed me and it was done.

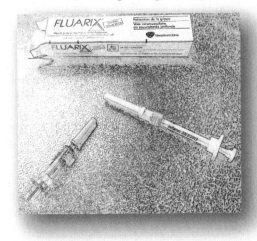

French friends were shocked when we told what we'd done. No, no, no, we were told. You take the syringe to your doctor. Or call for a nurse who will come to your home and inject you. Its free.

Woops.

Auxonne is in Bourgogne, about midway between the cities of Dole and Dijon, just a bit north of the most prolific wine area, where the best Burgundy wines come from. We were, the local Tourist Office told us, just 292 kilometers (181 miles) from the Eiffel Tower.

Auxonne is famous for its onions, although "famous" might simply be a polite expression, in the sense of "everybody is special in his own way" or "every place is famous for something." Onions don't hold quite the same panache as the world's best wines produced by Auxonne's more famous neighbors. As a result, the Auxonnoise have an inferiority complex, evidenced by the universal response when we told people we were Americans living on a boat in Auxonne for tout l'hiver, all the winter.

"Auxonne?," they'd say, a puzzled look on their faces. "Pourquoi Auxonne?"

Auxonne is a military town, known for its fortifications. It once guarded the boundary between France and the Austro-Hungarian Empire. The story goes that until recently professional barge folk navigating down the River Saone, where Auxonne is located, referred to the right bank, on the west, as "France" and the left bank, on the east, as "l'empire." Most of the fortifications still stand, although in various states of repair. We were moored right up against one section of these ramparts.

The French artillery school was located there. Its most famous graduate was a young lieutenant named Napoleon Bonaparte. Where we live in Massachusetts, unless your town has at least one building with a plaque confirming that "George Washington slept here" the town has no claim to be historic. Napoleon, it seems, slept around as much as did Washington. His statue looms over the town square beside the church. His name adorns everything from streets to pharmacies to bars.

While the famous artillery school has moved on, perched above our boat were the barracks for the 511th Regiment du Train of the French Army. I marched past these soldiers on my daily voyages to the boulangerie. They didn't appear to be doing much military but they look awfully martial in their camos and their tiny black berets perched on their foreheads.

I passed a sign next to the ramparts every day walking to and from the barge with a warning "Zone dangereuse defense d'entre pendant les tirs fanion en place." Out of curiosity, I plugged that into Google translate, which told me: "Danger zone. Forbidden to enter when the shooting pennant is in place." Interesting, as this was about a hundred feet from our boat. I never saw a shooting pennant.

We felt a special affinity with these soldiers since 500 of their predecessors in the Auxonne Artillery Regiment were critical to the ultimate American victory at the battle of Yorktown in the American Revolution. Reenactors still dress as Auxonne Artillery in the States. Coming from Ipswich, Massachusetts, where our town seal proclaims us as the birthplace of American independence - Ipswichers coined the phrase "taxation without representation" in a short-lived revolt in 1687, just five years before our neighbors in Salem started rounding up witches, including eleven folks from Ipswich - we take both the American Revolution and, even more so, reenactments of our local battles quite seriously. So, thanks to all you Auxonnoise soldiers.

The admiration is mutual. As appears to be universal in France, folks in Auxonne have a mystical image of New York City as equivalent to the Emerald City of Oz. On Auxonne's main street was a bar named Manhattan. A kebob shop named Happy Days featured New York's Chrysler Building on its sign. Our Tuesday night pizza shop – Star Pizza – was decorated with huge photos of New York. Incongruously, a hangout bar in town is the Cactus Cafe.

Auxonne isn't flashy, as is Paris with its wide avenues chock-a-block with upscale shopping. It isn't nearly as historic as Dijon, filled with ancient buildings and museums. It isn't as prosperous as its Burgundian wine neighbors. Streets fill with public school students, not oh so sophisticated university students. With the rental boat season long past, there were no tourists. We, and the handful of other boaters overwintering in the river port, were a perplexing anomaly.

But despite Auxonne's anonymity, or perhaps because of it, we had the time of our lives that winter. We met the most wonderful people: the retired Parisian lawyer who spent a day driving us through the rain to Dole and then translating for my cardiologist there, our boat neighbors who sold their farm and built the boat on which they travel the rivers, the hotel owner who let us use a meeting room for our weekly language get together and the women with whom we alternated French and English questions and answers, the oh-so-proper madame who softly commented, while shaking off her umbrella on a rainy afternoon that "il pleut comme vaches qui pissent" - it is raining like cows pissing, the Johnny Depp lookalike butcher where Sandra shopped, my boulangerie buddies who smiled as I butchered their language, the people who inhabited the pizza shop every Tuesday evening who took me into their circle and week after week were shocked that I was still in Auxonne, Sandra's internet pen pals who met her in Dijon before language lessons there, the family who dined on the boat and invited us to meet their friends. Maybe because Auxonne lacked flash, we became an item in town, the Americans on the boat spending the winter in Auxonne.

Pourquoi Auxonne, they all wondered.

Our response, because it is Auxonne, because it is France.

There is no "no" in Noël

Ah, the holiday season. In the States the season begins, appropriately, on Black Friday, the kickoff to the shopping Superbowl, or, to continue the sports metaphor, the "gentlemen, start your engines" to the Indianapolis 500 of consumption. Such competitive shopping may be part of the seasonal scene in Paris – although, since we were nowhere near Paris, we really have no idea – but out in the countryside the season is dictated by traditions as old as the hills. Here, the season of Noël, the French word for Christmas, centers on something more quintessentially French than spending money or gift giving. What is more important than frantic shopping for expensive gifts, you may ask.

Food.

Quelle surprise!

By the end of this month-long celebration, as we sprawled our way into January, we were up to our eyebrows in champagne and my blood had devolved to a cholesterol transportation system moving globs of foie gras from one organ to the next.

We were sated with Noël. Full to the brim. The past month had been, to paraphrase the Maine lobsterman's greeting as we sailed past him in pea soup fog, a mind-boggling experience . . . if we survive. Here's a summary of the month of Noël (leaving out the rain, fog, cold, wind, clouds, floods – yes, the river did a bit of rising – and Mordoresque gloom that overhangs France around the winter solstice).

Winter is dark here. Keep in mind that northern France is as far north as Newfoundland. The toasty Cote d'Azur, where we escaped a few weeks later to warm up, is north of our home in Ipswich, Massachusetts, which is covered in snow all winter. To brighten the darkest, longest nights of winter French cities evolved a tradition of les lumieres, illuminations, lighting up their downtowns in competitive megawatt displays. Northeastern France, where we spent the winter, is particularly known for its Christmas markets. Strasbourg has the oldest, at 451 years. The lumieres light up these Christmas markets.

We started with a train ride to Dijon for a combination of the lighting of its lights with the opening of the last of its new tram lines. Added in was a dinner with a couple of French families that turned into a grand crepe feast, initiated, as with seemingly every other activity this time of year, from solemn pageant to taking out the trash, with champagne and foie gras. The official color of the new Dijon trams is pink, exceptionally pinkish pink. Dijon's version of the Arc d' Triumph, rebuilt after a fire in 1137, was illuminated in pink.

Our initial holiday foray to Dijon merely placed our toes over the seasonal threshold.

Dijon was such fun that we decided to visit the highly touted Noël marché in nearby Montbeliard. We'd visited that city, located in the region of Franche-Comte, on the barge. The Montbeliard marché de Noël is a big one with 140 booths selling food and crafts. We spent three nights there, in a hotel carefully researched by Sandra to ensure the room had a bathtub. Food in Franche-Comte is basically different combinations of cheese and meat. Our first lunch, ordered at random from the menu, turned out to be round wooden boxes of Mont d'Or cheese, a pungent local cheese sold only in winter. The cheese was melted in the spruce box and surrounded by local sausages, a regional winter specialty. Sort of a fondue de cholesterol. Not surprisingly, my cardiologist has a thriving practice in Franche-Comte.

Waddling home on the train from Montbeliard back to the boat, the social season continued. Christmas was spent on a neighboring boat owned by a French couple. Sandra trades language lessons with Françoise; they had just finished a biography of Amelia Earhart, translating

French to English and English to French. Françoise prepared a Noël feast, starting with caviar and smoked fish, continuing through a traditional entre (what Americans would call the appetizer) of oysters, crevettes (shrimp) and snails (sea snails rather than land snails). Oysters at Christmas, you may ask. Christmas oysters are as essential to this French holiday as elves and Santas (although reindeer make no appearance in French Christmas). Wooden crates of oysters line the sidewalks. Shops that normally carry no food items have stacks of oyster crates. Our local tabac, which sells newspapers and cigarettes, (and gives away gossip for free), lined its sidewalk with stacks of wooden boxes filled with oysters. And they all disappeared. The French love their oysters, harvesting 287 million pounds per year; half that harvest is eaten between Christmas and New Years. We also had tournedos de boeuf, filet mignon, which, since it lacked that certain fatal level of cholesterol required for this season, was topped with foie gras.

Christmas dinner ended, of course, with its designated dessert, la bûche de Noël, the Yule log. Nothing wooden about this log. We'd been working our way up to the full bûche experience for a couple of weeks by buying a practice bûchette at the boulangerie to split for dessert. In French, a bûche is a log. A bûchette is a twig. Bûche de Noel is a big deal. I was at the patisserie when the Maître carried out the first tray of them, with a line of applauding customers out to the sidewalk. It is a spiral of sponge cake, chocolate buttercream, and secret stuff, frosted to look like a log, sometimes topped with powdered sugar snow. It sells in units of "persons:" 4, 6, 8, 10, 12 persons. A high-end Paris bûche designed by Givenchy goes for 160 euros. The high-end item at our Auxonne patisserie was the chocolate sanglier, a wild boar. But even the bûche de Noël is •modest compared with the traditional dessert in the south, in Provence, where they end the Noël meal with "treize desserts," thirteen desserts.

Then came New Years. We were invited to share New Years Eve with three French families in town, seventeen people all together. The email invitation began with the words "do not be afraid." We sat down at 8:00 p.m. and tried to stand up at 2:00 a.m. We vaguely remember about six bottles of different champagnes, interspersed with the appropriate local red and white wines for different courses, and won't ever forget the homemade foie gras on ginger and fig bread, a life changing experience in itself. It was an interesting walk back to the boat.

The next day, New Years Day, was a bargee party on a neighboring boat for all the folks overwintering at the marina.

As you could tell from that recitation, the holiday season in France is rich in tradition. And cholesterol. There is a specific baked product for each event. There is no saying "no" on holidays in which champagne and foie gras are prominent on most every menu. One tradition that is not readily apparent, however, is a religious one. Back in my days of working with the American Civil Liberties Union the surest signs of the holiday season's arrival were the law suits over placement of creches on public property and the question of whether they violated the U.S. constitutional mandate of separation of church and state. These cases were determined by applying a bizarre yet appropriately seasonal legal standard: the angels-to-elves ratio test. If the crèche was dominated by elves, it was secular and permissible. If angels played the lead roles, it was religious and con-stitutionally prohibited on government property. I've never seen a crèche in public in France. They are common inside churches, we're told, but public holiday decorations consist of trees, lights, colored balls and Santa.

French Santa looks just like American Santa (because he's the same person, right kids), although French Santa travels without any reindeer. And he is displayed climbing rope ladders and entering through windows, rather than down the chimney. Sometimes he travels incognito under the name of Père Noël, who has a donkey. Children leave out shoes filled with carrots for his donkey and get oranges back in the shoes in the morning. Unlike American Santa, whose job description includes deciding who is "naughty or nice" and awarding either toys or coal, a job that re-quires extensive year-long surveillance of American children - since taken over by the National Security Agency - French Santa is a complete good guy (unlike the NSA). Punishment duties are carried out by Santa's evil twin, Le Père Fouettard (the Bogeyman), who, covered in black coal, spanks naughty children. In neighboring Franche-Comte, Santa has a competitor from pre-Christian days, Tante Airie, who travels around with her friendly ass Marion. Both of them – Aunt Airie and Marion – showed up at Montbeliard.

The season ended with Epiphany, Twelfth Night, when we got to-gether on our boat with a French family to eat the appropriate cake for that day, the galette des rois, a pastry shell stuffed with frangipane, a mix-ture of butter, sugar, eggs, and ground almonds. The baker hides a charm - traditionally it is just a bean, but these days it is more likely to be a plas-tic figure of some kind - inside the cake. A child is supposed to hide un-der the table and decide who eats which slice of cake. Whoever gets the slice with the charm becomes king or queen for the day and wears the paper crown the baker provides with the cake. Sandra ordered our galette des rois at the patisserie and I picked it up that morning, standing in line with all the families picking up their galettes.

Our neighbor Phillipe found the surprise in his slice of galette. But wait, there's more; Sandra's slice also contained a prize, a tiny statue of the Virgin. We awarded her the crown and she was queen for the day.

Spending this holiday season in France, especially in small town France, was our holiday treat. We were so thankful to all the people who opened their hearts and their homes to us. Without a doubt, the best gift we could have received from this season was the gift we gave ourselves.

France.

The second best gift was a trip south to sun and warmth on the Cote d'Azur.

Visit to a Nice - rhymes with peace - hospital

Lying flat on my back on a hard, chilly sidewalk on a side street in Villefrance-sur-Mer on the sunny Cote d'Azur, some of the world's most expensive real estate, I gazed up at the blue sky. Two stories above me an elderly woman peered over her balcony. An American sprawled on the sidewalk, she thought. Haven't seen that in weeks. Then she continued sprinkling her azaleas, water overflowing from the planter and spilling onto the sidewalk below, gently splashing onto my head. Sandra sat next to me on a stone wall, dialing on her cell phone for the pompiers – the firefighters – to come in their ambulance to cart her husband off. Passers by

passed by until one young man walked up to Sandra, glanced at me lying on the sidewalk and began speaking to her in rapid French. Oh, thank you. I've called the pompiers, she replied. They are coming. He continued speaking rapidly, increasingly frustrated at her incomprehension until he held up an unlit cigarette and gestured. No, Sandra, replied. I don't have a light. He walked off in a huff.

We'd taken five weeks off the barge to warm up in the south of France, then Lisbon, and then on Madeira, an island off the west coast of Africa.

Soon, we heard the eeeee-ahhhhh, eeeeee-ahhhhh, eeeeee-ahhhhh of European sirens, the sound that in films indicates the Gestapo is closing in on Anne Frank. The siren faded in and out, first from the north, then the south, east, then west. Apparently, the ambulance was approaching in a spiral rather than directly. It arrived and out leapt three young pompiers in full uniform, ankle-to-neck blue jumpsuits, black boots, reflective tape covering at least a third of their outfits, backpacks, shoulder bags, suitcases, strange square black boxes, badges, insignia, caps, rubber gloves. Pompiers are a big deal in France, a big deal having little to do with fighting fires, or even driving ambulances. The primary job description of pompiers is to jog in unison through cities in packs of a half-dozen wearing skin-tight black tee shirts with matching and equally tight short shorts while fashionable women sip coffee at sidewalk cafes along their route sitting at strategically placed tables so they can comment on the merits and virtues, or lack of same, of the parading pompiers. A highlight of the social scene across France every Bastille Day is the local Bal des Pompiers, the Firemen's Ball. Unlike in the U.S., where the only number to dial in an emergency is 911, France presents a menu of emergency numbers. The universal number for any emergency is 112. For emergency medical help you dial 15, which gets you to SAMU, the nation-wide medical emergency system. For police, you dial 17. Nonetheless, we'd been told, although on reflection perhaps we'd been told mostly by Sandra's French women friends, no matter what your problem is, dial 18. That brings the pompiers. Hopefully by a vehicle and not by foot, in a pack.

The three pompiers stood in a circle around me and unpacked their equipment, preparing for a long stay. What was the problem, they asked. Probably that is what they asked. At least, none of them waved unlit cigarettes so they were not asking for a light. Sandra told them we'd been for a long walk. To see the Rothschild estate on Cap Ferrat, she said (although actually I had been more interested in locating Villa Nellcôte, the

159

mansion trashed by the Rolling Stones when they recorded Exile on Main Street there). We'd walked and walked and I became dizzy. Each time I became dizzy I sprayed a shot of the medication the cardiologist had prescribed for heart problems. Then I did what for me had historically been what induced cardiac distress; we visited an art museum, the Chapelle St-Pierre, a small church decorated floor to ceiling by Jean Cocteau. After all, it was a visit to the Boston Museum of Fine Arts that sent me to the Brigham and Womens Hospital cardiac emergency room almost two years earlier. Walking from the artistic church, I had to sit, then, sitting, I had to lie down. Sandra called the pompiers.

I was lifted into the ambulance and wrapped in a gold foil warming blanket, carefully tucked in until I looked, as one pompier commented, like a saucisson, a sausage.

That is what passes for ambulance humor in France.

Twenty minutes later we arrived at the Hospital Louis Pasteur in nearby Nice – a teaching hospital with a noted cardiac unit – and I was rolled into the emergency room. A nurse spoke some English and questioned me about what had happened. She took my medical history, including the Boston cardiology experience. Was I in any pain, she asked, now or when I'd been dizzy, especially any chest pain? No, I replied, no pain at all. She asked what I'd eaten during the day. She listened to my heart and took a drop of blood from a fingertip and tested it on a device. The doctor arrived and the two of them spoke, again in rapid French. I attempted to understand what they were saying. One phrase drew my attention. Pas de pain, they repeated to one another, apparently with great significance. Ah, I thought, "no pain," it means something important that I have no pain, that's good, I suppose. Last time I was at a hospital I had chest pain. Now I have none at all. Pas de pain, no pain. Good, I thought. The doctor repeated the phrase, questioningly, pas de pain? The nurse turned to me and said, in English, the doctor does not understand why you had no bread with lunch. Suddenly, I understood. "Pain," as in pas de pain, had nothing to do with pain – as in "pain in the neck" – but "pain" as in bread. Your blood sugar is low, the nurse said. You should eat bread. She gave me a cup filled with sugar water.

Because of my cardiac history – and my severe bread deprivation – the decision was made to admit me to the cardiac intensive care unit for observation. Observation and bread. Machines were connected. Tests were taken. Scans were done. Tubes were inserted. Interns, residents, medical students, cardiologists, nurses came and went. An American patient was an oddity and everybody wanted to visit. The resident had studied at Beth Israel Hospital in Boston. A cardiologist had spent three years at Brigham & Womens Hospital. They wanted to reminisce about Boston. A nurse was soon to vacation in New York. Did I have any restaurant suggestions? Another nurse was going to Miami and Orlando in a few months. Was Disneyworld wonderful? The radiologist was planning a trip to the U.S.. He wanted to see New York City, Texas and the Grand Canyon. Could he do that in one day, he asked? The nutritionist walked in carrying a clipboard. She looked at it with a worried expression and confirmed that, truly, I had eaten no bread with my lunch that day. You should eat bread, she said. Not surprisingly, every food tray delivered to my bedside for the next two days contained half a baguette.

We're keeping you overnight for observation, the cardiologist said. The next morning a tray was placed next to my bed with, voila, half a loaf of bread and a soup tureen containing some black liquid. No coffee cup. That was breakfast. Must be no caffeine in the cardiac unit, I thought, not even the thimble of coffee, all that gets served in French cafes. A tentative sip from the tureen, which took two hands to hold, revealed that the vat of black fluid was coffee, enough coffee to bathe in. Not surprisingly, my blood pressure, taken as soon as I'd slurped a liter of tepid coffee, had jumped. The tray was not removed until the last of the bread disappeared. Thus fortified, next came a stress test on a stationary bicycle, another test that disclosed no heart problems.

That was enough to have me ejected from intensive care and sent to a room with a roommate, a worried man who spent the day talking on his cell phone in Arabic, from time to time removing his hospital johnny and getting dressed and disappearing, gesturing that he was going outside for a smoke. He, it turned out the next morning, was having the battery changed in his pacemaker.

People came and went but identifying who was who in the hospital presented problems since there did not seem to be any system to the uniforms people wore. Perhaps they said who they were, but it flew by too quickly to understand. One woman who ordered me out of bed was not there to examine me, as I thought, but just to change the linen. A young man with two days' beard, torn jeans, a leather jacket and a motorcycle helmet who dropped into the room to chat turned out to be last night's cardiologist, on his way home.

The next morning resulted in more tests and more cardiologists all finding no problem. It was a mystery. Finally, one doctor asked about the spray I had used when I became dizzy. Had I taken this medication before, the doctor asked. I explained that I'd been given the same medicine, in small pills, back in the states and had been told that if I had heart problems I should take one pill, wait five minutes, take another if needed, wait five minutes and if I needed a third pill I should go to the hospital after taking it. Absolutely no more than three pills should be taken. Three pills had preceded my U.S. hospitalization. Arriving in France, a cardiologist had prescribed the spray rather than pills but said it was the same medicine. The day before in Villefranche, I explained, I'd taken three sprays. The doctor's eyes went wide. Three sprays, he said and explained that one spray is the dosage of three pills. I had taken the equivalent of nine pills. No wonder I couldn't stand up.

That could be the problem, the doctor said. More tests were done, all revealing no irregularities. It was decided to discharge me after two nights with a monitoring device connected to electrodes on my chest. This device would record 48 hours of heart rhythms. Come back in two days, I was told. And eat bread.

The next day, fully wired and recording, we took the train down the coast for 40 minutes to Italy, to the hilly town of Bordighera. I put my heart through the paces, climbing hills and walking all day, eating pasta and calamari. And drinking coffee, strong Italian coffee. Two days later I returned to Hospital Louis Pasteur, where the cardiologist spent a half hour reviewing the output from the monitor while I waited. I never made it to his office. He met me in the hallway.

You're fine, he said. You have no heart problems. Eat more bread. And he walked away to deal with sick people.

He seems to have been right. We spent the next two weeks in the warm sun of Madeira, off the west coast of Africa, doing hours-long hikes up steep mountain trails, without a hint of a problem. The wonders of medicine.

As a final note, three days at Brigham and Womens Hospital – admittedly one of the finest hospitals in the world, a Harvard teaching hospital – had resulted in a bill for $60,000 (yes, that is sixty-thousand dollars), fortunately covered by our U.S. medical insurance. Three days at a noted French cardiology hospital, with tests, medications and hot and cold running specialists, cost 3,200 euros, about $4,400. It was paid in full by our expat medical policy – the French health system doesn't cover us – a policy that costs for one year what our U.S. insurance costs for one month. The return visit, at which the cardiologist spent a half hour reading the cardiac monitor, cost another 34 euros, less than $50. That's what a U.S. hospital would charge for an aspirin.

I left with a prescription for exactly the same medications I'd been taking before the whole experience. Best of all, though, was doctor's orders.

Eat more bread.

An abundance of Burgundy

The next Spring, we were on the Canal du Centre in southern Bourgogne. It had rained for three weeks. The River Saone, which we'd left a few days before, was white water. Whole trees floated past us. The river banks were submerged so that we had to guess whether trees standing in what seemed the middle of the river were actually on the left bank or the right bank. We'd been relieved to escape the river and duck into the canal for a relaxed trip through southern Burgundy.

We ambled at the casual canal pace to our first mooring at Fragnes and settled into cruising mode, with white water racing, river flooding, navigation closures and white knuckles behind us and a summer cruise down the Loire Valley ahead of us.

Peace. Calm. Bliss. Wine. Cheese. Cows. Goats. Castles. Wine.

For a couple of days at least.

"So, what are you going to do while they repair the canal," asked an Australian couple on another barge.

"Repair the canal?" I responded. "What is wrong with the canal?"

It turned out that the day after we entered the Canal du Centre the heavy rain so saturated the ground that a wall ten kilometers ahead of us collapsed, dumping the canal onto a field and dropping a dozen boats into the mud. VNF, the Voies Navigables de France, the canal authority, predicted ten days to repair the breach. Nobody believed that prediction. It took ten days to begin work, and two days after beginning there were two national holidays. Predictions ranged from three to six more weeks before we could move on.

So we found a friendly canal bank to tie up to just below a lock in the village of Rully, surrounded by vineyards and restaurants, a four kilometer bike ride along the canal to Chagny, which had a good train connection. And that is where we spent nearly a month, running our generator a few hours a day to charge the batteries. Sandra planned our daily excursions by bike, bus and train, or by bike to the train station then with the bikes on the train to the nearby city of Chalon-sur-Saone and its bus station, then with the bikes on the rack at the back of the bus further south into Bourgogne to ride over hills and past farms, fields and vineyards through a countryside of medieval villages.

On one bike ride, a field filled with goats stood in front of a rambling farmhouse with a sign announcing chevre – goat cheese – for sale. We peddled up the dirt drive and knocked on the farmhouse door. The woman making cheese inside sold us three rounds she'd just made, and a bottle of Macon Village, then chatted for a half hour about dairy farming in France while Sandra described the farm at which she milked cows at home in Massachusetts.

American dairy farms are so large, the woman told us. How large is the farm where you milk, she asked Sandra.

Forty-six milking cows.

That is not so large, the woman replied, clearly disappointed. She expected an American farm to be an entire bovine metropolis.

Another day we planned to take a bus into Chalon-sur-Saone from the town of Fragnes but since it was a Saturday, the bus – which doubled as the town's school bus – was not running. Instead, the bus company provided a taxi for the usual bus fare of 1.50 euros. We got no farther into Chalon than a collection of tents that turned out to be the local Lions Club charitable gastronomy fair. Three euros bought you a wine glass on a loop of string that you wore around your neck as you walked from table to table sampling wines, cheeses and snails.

We met a pair of brothers from Savoie in the French Alps who bottled ice wine, made from grapes harvested frozen in December then helicoptered to 12,000 feet on the mountain to freeze solid for four days before the juice was pressed out, with the alcohol and flavors concentrated and the frozen water discarded. We left with a bottle of this concoction.

One day's excursion involved turning the boat around – a straight-forward U-turn – complicated by the fact that our 70-foot boat was in a canal that was 50 feet wide. Turning around involved a call to VNF to let them know what we were doing, which resulted in four men in two cars to oversee us, then motoring four kilometers up the canal through three locks to a wide spot where we could slowly turn around, then back four kilometers and three locks to the exact canalside spot from which we'd started, but facing now in the opposite direction. Two hours, eight kilometers, six locks, four supervisors. All to do an about face. See why our days were filled.

We knew we'd become part of the local scene when, after nearly two weeks tied to the same spot on the side of the canal, the local fishermen started chatting with us. One man, who I'd seen every afternoon tending his four side-by-side fishing rods for hour after hour, never catching a thing, walked over to chat one afternoon. It turned out he owned a bou-langerie in nearby Chalon-sur-Saone. Before getting married and becom-ing landlocked, however, he'd worked on French merchant ships sailing the world, serving as the bread baker on the ships. Who knew that all French ships carry a baker. He told us about baking bread for French soldiers going to fight in Indochina and Algeria, and of visiting Boston, New York, and Miami on ships. This was another conversation in which he assumed we were both fluent French speakers, never slowing down for more than a brief breath.

Best of all, most days during this waiting time we hopped on our bikes and pedaled to the vineyards that surround Rully, première cru Bourgogne vineyards making some of the world's finest wines. You knock on the door and are invariably invited in for a degustation, a sam-pling of their wines. At one vineyard – belonging to Jean-Claude and Anna Breliere – when we arrived Anna was under the hedges pruning as Jean-Claude walked into the yard grinning and inviting us inside. Two-and-a-half hours later we pedaled back to the boat and waited for Jean-Claude to deliver the twelve bottles we'd purchased. It took so long be-cause we had to sample our way through four different white wines and then five different reds, from ordinary Bourgogne (which was far from ordinary) up through their première cru. Just when we thought we were done, Jean-Claude pulled out two bottles with foil-covered corks. "Now for the cremants," he declared, pouring Burgundy's version of champagne. Fortunately, vineyards are on the hillsides and boat moorings are down in the valleys. All we had to do was coast home.

Once again, the wonders of living without a schedule and leaving yourself open for whatever happens turned what we'd planned as a four-day cruise through southern Burgundy into a four-week exploration of one of the most beautiful and enjoyable parts of France we've visited. The canal repairs would be finished, some time, and our travels would continue, some time. And once again, we were in pinch-me mode in the midst of France.

A typical barge day

We eventually gave up on waiting for repairs to the collapsed wall of the Canal du Centre. We'd planned a clockwise circle through a corner of northeast France. Instead, we turned the boat around and headed back down the canal, a short distance to the River Saone. We spent the night at Fragnes, our first stop on the canal.

Our plan was to get an early start the next day and buck the strong flood current on the river for a couple of days to get to the entrance to the Canal du Bourgogne and start a new counter- (you Brits would say anti-) clockwise loop.

People ask what we did all day on this barge thing? Come on now, what does anybody do all day? The day we left Fragnes was a fairly typical day, typically exciting, peaceful, frightening, pleasant, frustrating, fascinating and rewarding.

So, here is how the day went.

7:00 a.m. – Up early and walk to the boulangerie. They've been baking for hours. Bins are already packed with six different breads. Shelves are stocked with croissants and pastries. Madam Boulangére changes from town to town but they greet you with the same smiling "bonjour monsieur" every time you enter. Every boulangerie means a decision of what bread to buy today. A simple baguette, which will melt in your mouth if eaten in the next hour but by the end of the day will be fit only as swan food. Pain au cereal, French whole wheat bread, spongier but without that crunchy crust. Pain levain, sourdough bread that lasts for three days, if for some reason it isn't eaten before then. Or any of half a dozen others. Today its just a couple of baguettes. We'll eat them on the way. I exchange bonjours and chit chat before ordering two baguettes and two pains au chocolate, then we exchange bon journée , have a good day, with each other, then we reply to each other with à vous aussi, same to you, then au revoirs are exchanged. Finally I can turn and leave, but not without bidding bon journée to anybody standing in line behind me and accepting their à vous aussi in reply before I walk back to the boat.

7:15 a.m. – Brew some French coffee, download the New York Times (for me) and Le Monde (for Sandra) and finish our pains au chocolate. We ran outside and watched a dozen hot air balloons float overhead. There was a gathering of these balloons, which the French call "Montgolfiers," named after the brothers who invented them.

8:00 a.m. – On the way to Franges we'd passed a farm on the canal with a fenced-in yard filled with clucking chickens. That meant eggs would be for sale, and possibly fresh chickens. We walked down the road to the farm, bought a dozen eggs, the dirtiest, roughest-looking eggs I'd ever seen, covered in "stuff." But bright yellow yolks would be inside. Sandra asked the farmer if he had a chicken we could buy. Most were already reserved he said, but he had a few extras so we bought one. Is it fresh, she asked. Oh yes, he said. I just killed it yesterday afternoon. As a bonus, this farmer ran the distribution point for the local wine cooperative. Couldn't pass that up so we filled our folding shopping cart with a 5 liter bag of local red Bourgogne and half a dozen Cotes' de Nuit from a local vineyard. Then back to the boat.

8:30 a.m. – Check the oil and coolant in the engine, the gearbox oil and tension on all the engine belts, start the big Ford diesel and let it warm up for 10 minutes. Then untie the mooring lines, push off from the quay with our boat poles and motor down the canal to the big lock where the Canal du Centre meets the River Saone. This is an exceptionally deep lock. Most locks have swinging doors at either end, giant steel versions of the saloon doors you see in western movies. This lock has guillotine gates, steel plates that slide up and down on chains to seal off the ends of the lock. Sitting at the bottom of the lock chamber with the gates shut at either end, all you can see looking up is a slice of sky above you and slimy walls on both sides, rising 10.8 meters, 35 feet. After the water is drained

169

from the lock and the boat settles down to the level of the river, the chains rattle and the gate in front of the boat lifts. You motor out under the gate and face the River Saone. Actually what we faced was a four-man rowing shell drifting right in front of the lock. It's a tossup who was more surprised, us or them. They scuttled out of the way and we motored onto the river.

9:30 a.m. – 2:00 p.m. – We motored up the Saone. The whole reason for this about face and change of plans was that all the rain had washed out the Canal du Centre in front of us and filled the River Saone behind us, making river navigation questionable. By this time, however, the river had begun dropping and we decided that a couple of days motoring up-river into the current was the lesser of the evils and was safe, even if it would be slow. It was safe. It was slow. The good part was that we got to rev the diesel engine high enough to clean away whatever deposits had built up inside. Diesels like to be run hard and by the end of the day we had a smiling diesel. And a hot one. Since one of the ways we heat water in our hot water tank is by running the engine coolant through a coil in the tank, by the end of the day we had lots of exceptionally hot water.

While I steered the boat upriver, Sandra spread our farm chicken on a cutting board on the wheelhouse table and cut it into pieces, preparing a coq au vin to marinate in the wine we'd bought at the farm. We both paused for a vegetarian moment when she held up the chicken's heart and said, "this was beating yesterday." We paused for only a brief moment, though. Friends had called from the train at Lyons. They were on the way to their boat at St. Jean des Losne, where we were heading, and would join us onboard for dinner the next night. The coq au vin needed a night to marinate. The vegetarian moment gave way to anticipation of a fine meal.

On we motored against the current, making surprisingly good progress.

2:00 p.m. – We'd decided to break the trip upriver to the entrance to the Canal de Bourgogne into two days. This same trip had taken us five hours downriver, traveling with the current, a few weeks earlier. Around 2:00 p.m., past the halfway point, we started looking for a place to moor for the night. We were topped up with water. Running all day filled our battery banks. We had plenty of food on board. We'd bought two baguettes in the morning, and lots of wine. All we needed was a safe place to tie up out of the current. It took four tries.

First attempt – We only had two locks on the river to pass through, big locks, though, hundreds of feet long, capable of serving the huge commercial boats on the river. The Viking cruise ships you see advertised on Public Broadcasting in the States. These modern locks, with the eclusiers – the lockkeepers – perched in a glass control tower high overhead, replaced older, smaller locks. The old abandoned locks can be entered from the downriver end and used as temporary overnight moorings. We passed one and planned on staying in the second one, just below the town of Seurre. Our chart book has a photo of a little cruising boat sitting "dans l'ecluse desaffectee' de SEURRE," which we translated as "in the disused lock at Seurre." Four fairly-well inebriated fisherman were huddled around a campfire on the river bank in front of l'ecluse desaffectee'. They were assigned that location by the French government. Every time you do something stupid on a boat there are official observers, part of François Hollande's full employment plan. They cheered us on as we motored toward the old lock. And cheered even louder as we ground to a halt in a flurry of bottom mud churned up by our propeller. We'd run aground. Fortunately, at full throttle, we were able to inch backwards out of the mud. Obviously, the lock had filled in since the photo of the cute little cruiser was taken. The official observers waved farewell as we motored away.

Second attempt – Our chart showed a set of long stone stairs, about 100 meters wide, on the riverfront in Seurre, an arrangement commonly used as a mooring location. Half of this length had a sign saying it was reserved for a restaurant boat. The other half was wide open. We hung our tire fenders over the side and inched our way toward the steps. Unfortunately, the river was so high that the lower few steps were under water. We bumped into them and came to a stop, a meter or more of water-filled space separating our boat from the first above-water step. Sandra – wisely – balked at making the leap with the mooring lines. We were concerned that if we tied up above these submerged steps and the river went down over night, we'd come to rest on the stone steps, not to float again until the next flood. On we motored, but not before waiving at the half-dozen elderly official government screw-up observers taking careful, nodding note of our efforts.

Third attempt – The Dutch Barge Association cruising guide for Seurre said there was a floating pontoon, upriver from the steps, run by a commercial operation. We reluctantly decided to pay the 21 euro fee the guide listed. An outrageous amount. More than we'd ever paid. But, any port in a storm, or flood. The far end of the floating pontoon was empty and we motored up to it, only to see a strip of police tape and a large "reserve"' sign. No, no, no the official observers, a different set of them, muttered. (A year later, on a return to Seurre, we learned that the "reserve" sign was a permanent fixture and could be freely ignored.)

Fourth attempt – OK, we decided we'd just create a wild mooring, an unofficial, ad hoc place along the river where we would tie up. We went through the Seurre lock, like a water-filled football field, motored on a few hundred meters and clamped on to the corrugated steel plates that formed the side of the industrial stretch of canal there. We have a pair of heavy iron clamps designed to screw onto these steel plates, which are commonly used to hold up canal banks. The clamps have a ring welded on their sides to which we attach our mooring lines. We'd never used these clamps before, but this was a fine time to test them. Seeing no official government observers was a good sign we would not face another disappointment. We rested the boat against the canal siding, slid our clamps in place, attached our mooring lines and, voila, we were safely moored for the night. Patience, perseverance, ingenuity and a boatload of friendly nods to the observers of disasters had prevailed.

3:00 p.m. – We climbed off the boat and walked downriver to the town of Seurre, which turned out to be an interesting place with lots to see, especially a café with sidewalk tables, offering a list of local wines by the glass. We asked if there was a market in town and the café owner directed us to a store, 10 minutes walk away. A quick shopping trip for mushrooms for the chicken and ice cream for dessert and we walked back to the boat, hauling ourselves and our groceries over the steel pilings to which we'd moored.

7:00 p.m. – We barbecued hamburgers with the remains of the morning's baguette for dinner, along with a sweet potato from the grocery and cole slaw Sandra made from a red cabbage we'd bought from the farmer. We tapped the bag of wine we'd bought and had dinner at the wheelhouse table with rain, rain and more rain falling around us.

So, that is what a day on the barge is like. Food, finding it, preparing it, eating it, is a large part of our day, shopping in the morning for what we eat at night, as do the French. Handling the boat as a team is another large part of what we do, sometimes things going smoothly, sometimes putting on a show for the official observers of screw-ups. And discovering unexpected bits of France is part of every day, the farmer selling us the chicken he'd raised and killed yesterday, a sky full of Montgolfiers, the guillotine lock, the 5 kilometer an hour current in the river, the first time use of our mooring clamps. And a small slice of the River Saone all for ourselves for the night.

La Loire, where your castle is your home

We circled through the Loire Valley, a region in which we'd been promised our fill of chateaux - castles - alongside three canals: Loing, Briare and the sonorous Canal Lateral a la Loire. This was a new region of France, new for us, old for France, of course. We found cities with musical names: Nemours. Montargis. Chatillon-Coligny. Briare. Sancerre. La Charite-sur-Loire. Nevers. Digoin.

The lesson of the Loire was that France is so much more than Paris. In fact, France and Paris are two separate, distinct experiences, as different as New Mexico and New York. You've no more experienced France if you've only been to Paris than you've experienced the United States if you never strayed beyond Times Square. Even if you also dropped in at Disneyworld. If you've never been to Paris, drop everything and go there, along with the 27 million or so annual tourists who will elbow you in the ribs to glimpse the diminutive Mona Lisa. But my advice is that once you've seen Paris, escape it and see the rest of France. That's what the French do.

The Loire is a fine place to begin seeing Not-Paris, France. The Loire is the Mississippi River of France, its longest river, but not its friendliest for boats. There was a long period in which the Loire was so difficult for boats that the practice was to cobble together wooden barges well up the river, fill them with stuff to sell in the big cities, float them down the river, then break the boats apart and sell them as firewood rather than try to drag them up the shallow Loire. Technology intervened to end that practice when the Canal du Centre – connecting central France with the Loire – was opened in 1793. Things got even better when the Canal Lateral a la Loire – the canal alongside the Loire – opened in 1838. This canal allowed boats to pretty much avoid the sandy Loire entirely and, connecting to the older Briare (1642) and Loing (1660) canals, opened the door for Burgundy wine to float to the Seine and on to Paris, and for the barges to float back again.

We took advantage of this technology dating from 1642 to 1838. It was startling to realize that we were being lifted by canal locks built fifty years before the folks at home in nearby Salem, Massachusetts got around to hanging the town's witches. Many of these locks use the same technology as when they were built: somebody – also-known-as-Sandra on our boat – pushes, pulls, lifts or turns a lever, an arm, a crank or a wheel that lifts, drops, opens or closes the doors at either end of the lock to fill it with water or let the water out. No motors involved.

We saw our fill of chateaus, what in England would be called castles. The older chateaus are King Arthur-style with towers, turrets, walls, drawbridges, moats. They probably had dragons. They did have dungeons. More recent, or more-recently renovated chateaus are more rightly just mansions, forsaking the military defenses for extravagant luxury. They tend to be quirky. Some examples:

The chateau at La Bussiere, near Gien, was owned by a noble family that included generations of obsessive fishermen. Room after room after room after room of the present version of the chateau is, pardon the term, stuffed to the gills with fishing ephemera. Every version of fishing rods cast by fishermen from Cro-Magnon to Hemingway. In fact, there is a stuffed coelanthis, a prehistoric fish long thought extinct, but not quite so. There is specialized fish-eating cutlery and plates, again, through the ages. Fish art covers the walls. Fish cooking items fill the chateau kitchens. And, naturally, or actually, not at all naturally but rather man made, the entire chateau is surrounded by a lake that to this day is stocked with fish and fished regularly by French prime ministers, sometimes by simply dangling a line from the porticoed balcony overlooking the lake. There's a great little restaurant in town, too, l'Insolite, inexpensive and worth the visit in itself. We had the fish menu of the day.

At the other extreme was the fortress-like chateau at St. Brisson sur Loire, near Briare. We saw a poster advertising a demonstration of machines de guerre of the Moyen Ages in the castle moat. Not something to be missed. A guy event if ever there was one, which pretty much describes the whole Middle Ages (which were sort of humanity's mid-life crisis, with inquisitions and crusades instead of blondes and sports cars). This was my reward for being dragged to view hundreds of murky oil paintings of saints and angels. We mounted our bicycles, pedaled up the hill on which the chateau was perched – nobody built castles anyplace down low – and arrived in time to see a troop of five men dressed in yellow and red robes, iron helmets on their heads, chain mail on their chests, pikes upon their shoulders and, perhaps a drop or two of wine in their bloodstreams, march across the drawbridge and down into the moat. Arranged in the moat was a collection of devices for, to put it simply, throwing heavy stuff a long way. Catapults. Trebuchets. Even a rudimentary cannon. Accompanied by much shouting, foot stomping, marching about and counting down in French, along with heads-up warnings to Jacques, hidden away far down the hill and through the woods, these Monty Pythonesque warriors loaded boulders onto the devices' various slings, pockets and boxes and launched them, not quite into orbit, but a long, long way into the unseen distance, followed by thuds and crashes and broken branches down the hillside.

A narrator told us the trebuchet was used not only to toss stones against castles, but also to "return" prisoners and peace emissaries over the walls. And the occasional diseased cow. Inspired, I decided I would recruit like-minded Ipswich-ites to build a trebuchet as a winter project when next we returned home. The Trustees of Reservations, owners of the "chateau" at Castle Hill at Crane Beach, should be warned.

It's a guy project.

Other non-chateau architectural wonders presented themselves on this canal loop. Although the canal traveled alongside the Loire for most of its way, the canal crossed the river in two places. In earlier days the river crossing was dependent on (1) the river having enough water for boats to cross and (2) the river not having too much water for boats to cross. The Goldilocks dilemma of too-much-water or too-little-water often blocked navigation for weeks. The solution was to build bridges across the river, bridges for boats. We motored the barge on bridges over the Loire in two places: Briare, at one end of the canal and Digoin at the other end. Picture the George Washington Bridge with a long bathtub rather than a roadway and a 70-foot barge rather than cars and trucks motoring down the bridge. No tollbooths, though.

At the other technological extreme from 350-year-old canals were a couple of French nuclear power plants located scenically canalside. Some places where we'd tie up for the night charged a small amount for us to plug in to electricity. Moorings at nuclear sites gave it away free. France gets 79 percent of its electricity from nuclear power, a greater percentage than any other country. There is absolutely no relationship between the ubiquity of nuclear plants and the odd circumstance of it never seeming to get totally dark at night anywhere we've moored.

The Loire, as with most regions of France, offered its local food and cheese and wine. The medieval town of Sancerre, naturally located at the top of a steep hill, was surrounded by vineyards making white wine of the same name. We rode our bikes to the base of the hill and then chained them up, daunted by its steepness. We asked at a bar whether there was a footpath up the hill. The proprietress walked us to the edge of the woods and pointed upwards. As we set off up a narrow dirt path we heard her shout a warm "bon courage" to us. We found a vineyard located a bit lower down the slope to make our purchases.

The Basilica of St. Magdelene at Vezelay is a UNESCO World Heritage site and, for almost 1,000 years, a destination for medieval pilgrims, now known as tourists. Our sincere young Audrey Hepburn look-alike tour guide at the cathedral, after pointing out the statues of "alien beings from other planets" on the church entrance, told us how fortunate we were to visit on the one day each year the gold box containing a 12 centimeter piece of Mary Magdalene's rib was removed from the crypt below the church. At least they are pretty sure it is really her rib, the guide told us.

A chance encounter with a family living alongside the canal at La Chapelle Montlinard directed us to follow an old dirt path up a hill at sunset to see an 800-year-old oak tree, surrounded by cows. The legend is that Joan of Arc stood under that tree looking at the medieval city of La Charitee-sur-Loire and swore that she would conquer that rebellious city the next day. Her army's failure was the first step on her path toward being burned at the stake.

I stood under that same tree, looked at the same city walls, and felt a connection with history, a connection with France, that sent chills down my back.

177

Three fantastic reasons why you should never, ever brag about how the engine has never, ever failed

Back in my newspaper reporter days one of the fundamental axioms of journalism was that things – fires, school bus crashes, tornadoes, insurrections, decapitations, everything – come in threes. If every structure in a village in India is inundated by a spontaneous plague of diuretic sparrows, well, put up your window screens. Two more swarms of tummy-troubled sparrows will coalesce somewhere on Planet Earth in the next week or so. Copy editors would automatically

start preparing headlines: Burb Braces for Third Bird Barrage.

Take my word for it. Things happen in threes. Scientific fact. Einstein predicted it. String Theory supports it. Its true.

So, at the beginning of our fourth summer in France, when the trusty Ford diesel in Hoop Doet Leven started overheating after two weeks in southern Burgundy on the Canal du Centre, I practiced my mechanical mumbo jumbo to deal with the engine. But I braced myself for what was certain to come next.

And next.

After all, it was my own fault. A week earlier, regret had set in the instant these words left my mouth. "We've never had a problem with the engine. Never a breakdown. Never a lost day. And all I do is change the oil and the filters. We've been so lucky."

Ah, how the Engine Gods must have grinned at that.

And how clever and sneaky, playful and clever - and nasty - they are when they set out to have fun.

Three hours of slow motoring past vineyards and fields had me well settled in that French mellow mode that brought us here. In and out of locks. A slight cross breeze to make barge handling interesting. The chugga chugga chugga of the exhaust stack sounding perfect. But wait. What is this? Sitting in our tenth lock of the day, waiting for the water to drop us to the level of the next section of canal, the temperature gauge started climbing. Odd. I left the lock, increasing the throttle to our canal cruising speed of seven kilometers an hour (about 3.5 miles an hour) and the temperature dropped to its normal level. Hmm. Strange.

At the next lock the same thing happened. Hotter though. The slower the engine turned the hotter it got. The faster it turned, the cooler. In our own speeded up version of global warming, the engine got hotter and hotter at each lock. And not nearly as cool in between.

It got serious. Eventually, we had to pull over and let the engine cool for an hour. Twice. We managed to arrive at Parray-le-Monial, the town where my visiting crew Jon was to leave and Sandra was to return from grandmother duty. Yes, Sandra was to arrive on a boat with, for the first time, engine trouble.

Should I tell her it was all my fault?

Not in quite those words, I decided. Not in quite any words, actually. But she assumed it was my fault.

It usually is.

Overheating is relatively simple to address. It can only be two things. Too much heat in the engine. Or not enough cool in the engine. I did my stuff. Adding a this. Removing a that. Changing one of those. Whatever I could think of.

And it was fixed.

But I knew that was just the first course, the interesting entrè at dinner before your plate principal arrives. Or maybe it was just the amuse bouche, the chef's freebie treat designed to delight your taste buds before the meal begins.

What would it be? What were the Engine Gods rubbing their hands in anticipation for?

The next morning, I slowly pulled away from our mooring and headed for a lock, Sandra at the bow. I put my left hand on the throttle lever and slipped it back to idle. Lined up the bow for the center of the rapidly approaching lock entrance. Slid the throttle into reverse.

And we didn't slow down. The throttle lever has a hole into which a metal shaft is inserted. Through magic, that shaft is connected to cables that control how fast the engine turns. Same lever controls the gear shift. Push the throttle forward and the boat goes forward. Pull it back and the boat reverses. Stand it straight up in the middle and the engine idles in neutral.

Usually.

This time the throttle lever just spun like a pinwheel on that metal shaft. The boat traveled no faster. No slower. No forward. No reverse. And certainly no neutral. Just 65 tons of barge driving straight for the stone and steel of a canal lock.

I shut the engine off and we drifted to a stop, well before the lock. I eased the boat to the canal bank. Sandra hopped off with a sledge hammer and our metal mooring stakes and we tied to the bank while I cogitated. This was a pretty simple problem, right?

A problem that was not entirely unanticipated. The metal shaft that goes into the shift lever has a series of splines at its end. Spline. Sort of like "spine." Raised metal ridges ringing the inch at the end of the shaft.

The hole in the shift lever has a series of grooves, grooves that, coincidentally, match the raised ridges in the shaft. The "splines" on the shaft slide into the "grooves" in the hole in the lever. Moving the lever rotates the shaft. There is a little setscrew at the bottom of the lever that holds things in place.

Remember this word "splines." It will assume monumental, and expensive, importance in a few days.

Splines.

I'd been tightening that teeny setscrew for some time as the throttle lever had become more and more squishy on its shaft. More and more play as I moved the lever before anything happened in relation to the engine. As I mentioned, this was not a totally unanticipated problem.

And it was easily remedied with one of the three essential tools of navigation, tools used by the Phoenicians to explore the Mediterranean and by both the Vikings and Columbus to cross the Atlantic. I deployed these tools in order of logic. I wanted the shaft to turn. I sprayed it with WD-40. No luck. I wanted the lever to be attached to the shaft. I wrapped it in duct tape. Still no luck.

So I gripped the shaft with my largest pair of vice grip pliers. Clamped it to the shifter shaft. Voila. I had a new, fully functional shift lever.

We set off once again.

Two problems down.

One to go.

The gates in front of us opened slowly in our third lock of the day. I aimed the bow at the center of the opening and eased the vice grip pliers slightly forward. And heard a screech like a coffee can filled with marbles being shaken by a deranged monkey. Vice grips back to neutral and the sound stopped. Vice grips into reverse and the monkey went crazy again. Neutral. Silence. Forward. The monkey returns. Throughout this crescendo the boat stayed in the center of the lock.

The lock tender looked down at the barge calmly as if this sort of thing happened every day.

I climbed off the boat with a rope over my shoulder and tugged us out of the lock and, once again, we staked out on shore.

I had a suspicion this third engine problem would require more than WD-40, duct tape and vice grip pliers. Besides, I only had one set of vice grips and they were already being put to use. We were tied to the canal bank, far from anything city-like, with an engine that no longer over-heated, with a throttle made from a pair of pliers but functioning just fine, but with an engine and gear box shrieking what I dreaded was its death rattle.

A Swiss couple we'd met cruised out of the lock and offered to tow us to the next town. It had a boulangerie. We would not be without bread while we solved our problem at least. It was a short distance. With no locks. Hoop Doet Leven reluctantly became a typical American dumb barge, towed from place to place by a real boat.

Fortunately, when I was back in problem No. 1 mode, the overheating engine, I'd come across Entente Marine, a boat yard run by two Brits just 20 kilometers and nine locks farther down the canal from where we'd ground to a halt. I got on the phone with them and one of the Brits showed up in his van. He quickly diagnosed the problem as the gearbox. Better than the engine I supposed. But we had to get the boat to his shop.

Can you tow us there, I asked. Hmm, he mumbled. I'd tow you in my boat but its engine isn't working. Could be the water pump. Not a propitious omen, I thought, keeping the thought to myself. Maybe you can get a passing boat to tow you, he suggested, none too helpfully.

We telephoned our Swiss friends, who'd moved on down the canal an hour earlier, and explained our situation. They turned around and re-turned to us. For the next two days, they towed us – actually they tied on to our side – for 20 kilometers and nine locks. A hundreds meters before each lock they untied from us and launched us toward the lock opening. Sandra steered into the lock as the barge's momentum carried it forward while I sat at the bow, rope in hand, legs out, ready to jump to the lock wall and drag the boat into the lock. Once the lock lowered us down, I put the rope over my shoulder and trudged along the shore, dragging the barge out of the lock and down the canal until they could reattach their boat.

Nine times.

This was horribly improper, my towing the barge by marching along the tow path, rope over my shoulder. Wrong. Historically incorrect. Not the way things used to be done on the canals.

Pulling a barge is woman's work, you see. In pre-engine days, the barge-husband stood at the wheel, smoking, steering. Captaining. The barge-wife, wearing her leather towing harness, pulled the boat. Truly. We've seen photos.

I was not about to suggest that Sandra don her leather towing harness.

So I pulled the barge. Slowly.

After two days of this we glided to the mooring at Entente Marine at Gannay-sur-Loire, a town large enough to have a boulangerie. And a cafe. A nice cafe. With a bottomless bottle of pastis. And a proprietor with a sense of humor. At lunch one day he placed a bowl of mustard in front of me, for my frites. "This eez French ketchup," he said.

Unfortunately, sometime in the history of the transformation from working barge to a floating home, our gear box, sitting between the engine to its front and the propeller shaft at the rear, was covered with the aft cabin shower stall. To get at the gear box, something, either the shower stall or the engine, would have to be removed. We opted for the engine.

Fortunately, the boat yard has a huge crane. And the roof of the wheelhouse, under which the engine lurks, is easily removable. As is the wheelhouse floor. When the engine was hoisted up and the gear box was examined the problem became instantly evident.

Test time. What was the word you I asked you to remember?

Splines.

It seems that running down the center of the gear box is the gear shaft. This shaft goes forward into a hole in the center of a two-foot-wide metal disc, a disc that moves back and forth to connect the gear box with the engine. Sort of like the clutch in a standard transmission car. And how does this gear shaft match up with this disc?

You've got it. Splines.

The end of the gear shaft is ringed with steel ridges. Splines. The hole in the disc is circled with grooves. The splines fit into the grooves.

The mad monkey sound we'd heard was the shaft undergoing a splineectomy, shearing off the grooves in the disc. Tossing a whirlwind of splines into the gear box.

But parts were available, somewhere in Europe. Rebuilding the old gearbox would cost almost as much as installing a new gear box so we opted for a new one. While the engine was out we chose to follow a suggestion made by our surveyor when we bought the boat. The engine was mounted directly to the hull, he'd said. Bad practice. It should be on flexible engine mounts. With a flexible coupling between the gearbox/engine and the propeller shaft. Is that important, I'd asked him.

If you don't do it you might need a new gearbox some day, he'd warned. We hadn't followed his advice. (NOTE: If you are looking for a barge surveyor, Barrie Morse obviously knows what he's doing.)

We - or at least Hoop Doet Leven - spent five weeks at Entente Marine at Gannay-sur-Loire as a new PRM hydraulic gearbox slowly wended its way from England, joined by a flexible motor mount (one, the only one in England it appears). Three more motor mounts were delivered from the Netherlands. A new gearbox plate, appropriately splined and grooved, was built, somewhere in Europe, just for us.

But it was France, land of savoir-faire, "know-how." Everything worked out. Eventually. And we kept busy. We spent a day riding our bikes to a hilltop medieval village, Bourbon Lancy, that was reputed to have a fantastic crepe house. Forty-five kilometers over rolling hills for crepes seems extreme. But they were great crepes. We rented a little hybrid Toyota Auris at just $100 a week. Before handing me the keys, the rental guy, eyeing Sandra and being French enough to know one does not embarrass a man in front of his woman, took me aside and quietly asked, "Do you know how to operate an automatic transmission." We visited English friends who bought a huge house in a tiny village in the Morvan, a mountain region in Burgundy. They've created the archetypical rural French refuge that is the subject of thousands of daydreams and fantasies. And a few books.

Driving through the Morvan we entered a small town and were surrounded by American soldiers who looked like they'd stepped out of "Saving Private Ryan." They were French reenactors of the U.S. Army from WW II, complete with jeeps, halftracks and a tank. They were shocked when I asked what they were celebrating. "But monsieur, today is the sixth of June," I was told. D Day. I told them my father had landed at Omaha Beach. They asked us to lead the parade. And they asked me to thank him.

As the repairs dragged on, Sandra took off for five days at a language school in a nearby town called Sancerre. They make a nice white wine there. Of course she studied hard.

But Gannay-sur-Loire, pretty much in the center of France, rapidly lost its charm. It had a grocery, but madame there was surly, not surly in the friendly French manner of you don't exist until you say bonjour but surly in the shoes-way-too-tight way. The Gannay boulangerie opened at random. And had bread even more randomly. The cafe owner's "French ketchup, ha, ha, ha" joke was not quite so funny the fifth time.

We scoured the map for places off the canals we'd want to visit. One treat was the city of Bourges, a historically (as if most everything in France is not in some way historic) capital of, at various times, the department of Cher, the former province of Berry, the Roman province of Aquitaine, and, during the reign of King Charles VII, of the kingdom of France. Nice cathedral. Lots of restaurants and cafes. Friendly people. Not inundated with tourists. And a restaurant, Entre Nous, that was so good at lunch we returned for dinner. The waiter recommended a local wine – pinot gris by Denis Jamain from Reuilly – that blew our socks off. Following our usual practice, we eventually tracked down M. Jamain, arranged a rendezvous at his vineyard and purchased several cases. The only problem was distinguishing between the pronunciation of this new wine – Reuilly – from a previous favorite in Burgundy – Rully. Pas de problème, we were told. "Reuilly" is pronounced "roo-ee." "Rully", on the other hand, is pronounced "roo-ee." See why France can be challenging.

The repairs dragged on, not at all the fault of the hard-working guys at Entente Marine. Lets just say that Vetus, a parts supplier, seemed to supply parts, but not necessarily the same parts we'd ordered, at moments of its own choosing. UPS, the ubiquitous worldwide shipper conveniently provides tracking numbers that allow you to follow your motor mounts as they make the grand tour of Europe; if its Tuesday our motor mounts must be in Düsseldorf. Our new clutch plate sent a postcard from Athens.

Three weeks into the process we drove to the Dordogne in the southwest of France.

Are you familiar with the game duck, duck, goose? That was the menu throughout the Dordogne. When you'd had your fill of duck at lunch, you were presented with a vast cross section of goose dishes for dinner. And both duck and goose foie gras. And tours of the duck farms. And the goose farms. But we did get to visit 17,000 year old cave paintings. Which made it all worthwhile.

Finally, five weeks into the repair process, all was coming together. Our motor mounts arrived from Holland, via the U.K. and Düsseldorf. All was installed. Friends from home who had expected to visit us on the barge instead drove from castle to chateau with us through the Loire Valley. We changed our cruising plans for the rest of the summer, putting off the Marne and Champagne until next summer. Instead, we would see how far south we could go on the Saone, toward Lyon, before returning, once again, to Auxonne for the winter.

We were confident it would all work out soon enough.

I told everybody we weren't concerned, expostulating at length about how disasters never come in fours.

Right?

Pulling the plug on France, temporarily

So much for smarmy, self-congratulating dissertations about how disasters always came in threes. Predicting that after we'd survived our third problem - the destruction of our spline-challenged gearbox - the rest of the summer would be awash in pain au chocolat and pinot noir was a prime example of my Pollyanna pipe-dreams preempting Sandra's cautious pessimism. Oh, foolish pride. Oh, what hubris. (But this was nothing new; we'd named the catamaran on which we'd planned on circumnavigating, "Catharsis").

Remember all my folderol about bad news coming in threes? Well, never mind. As I used to say in the heat of trial when the wrong phrase came from my mouth, "may that be stricken from the record, Your Honor" (which resulted, when the judge muttered "allowed," in the trial transcript not being purged of the misspoken words at all but, rather, including my original words plus the whole "strike that" interchange in the written record).

Let me tell you about the fourth – and final – surprise the barge had for us that summer.

An email from the mechanics with the subject line "Bad News" can't be good news. All the bits and pieces had arrived, they said. All the bits and pieces were installed, they said. The engine started right up and ran like clockwork, we were informed.

For ten minutes.

It seemed that in removing the engine from the boat with their giant crane, at various moments it had to be twisted, spun, turned on its side, turned on its end, rotated, inverted and do-si-doed to gyrate out of the engine compartment. Sometime in that process a small – but not too small – bolt that had rested innocuously, and loosely, in the deep recesses of the engine was roused from its years, nay, decades of slumber. This loose bolt was sucked into cylinder number six of the engine. Where piston number six rammed said bolt into shrapnel. Sort of like a hand grenade going off. Inside the engine. Yuck.

This repair would take a while, we were told. Maybe a few months. A French machine shop would have to remove the piston. An English engine shop could supply parts. Engine components would be visiting the obscure tourist destinations the motor mounts had missed.

That was it for us. We tossed in the towel and flew home three days after receiving the latest news. Summer Number Four barging in France was over.

Rediscovering America

We flew back to the United States on September 11. I know, not a propitious day for flying but, on the other hand, the airlines have to lower their fares to induce people to board planes that day. And we flew on Icelandair, with a stop in Reykjavik. Icelanders are kindly, fun loving, innocuous folks, not likely to work their way too high up on terrorists' next-ones-to-terrorize list. Although Iceland was included on the list of W. Bush's Coalition of the Willing to deprive Sadam Hussein of his nonexistent weapons of mass destruction, it turned out that only a single Icelander was actually willing to go to Iraq. (Check the YouTube video "The Loneliest Icelander." You can find this paean to one soldier at http://www.youtube.com/watch?v=dk4rBQDxOEE, featuring the patriotic poster urging Icelanders to "Support Our Troop.") So we made it back to Ipswich, Massachusetts (the "Other Ipswich" to you Brits, who keep reminding us that you have one also. Our Ipswich is next to Essex, near Gloucester, Rowley, and Manchester. Our kids live in Dover, Cambridge and Portland. Trying to figure out Massachusetts's geography makes the Queen's subjects dizzy.)

To prepare for our departure from France and re-injection into America, I scribbled checklists, such as this one:

"Things To Remember When Returning to the United States:"

- Americans believe in their heart of hearts that the United States is the Greatest Country in the World. Americans become upset if told they are wrong.

- The French believe in their heart of hearts that everybody else in the world believes that France is the Greatest Country in the World. The French become upset if told they are wrong.

- In America when a store has a sign saying it is open seven days a week, it is open Sundays.

- In France when a store has a sign saying it is open seven days a week, it is closed on Sundays. And maybe Thursdays. And Tuesday morning. And August.

- In America, unlike in France, it is not considered polite, when entering a doctor's waiting room, to kiss everybody sitting in the room. Or to shake their hands. Or even to make eye contact.

- At home, it is safer to walk down stairs facing forward, unlike on the barge.

- Dogs are not welcome in restaurants in America. Even if they can order for themselves from the menu.

- In France dogs are all over restaurants. Sometimes they have their own tables. With very low chairs. The drinking age for dogs in restaurants is two years. We were in a fairly formal restaurant when a waiter brought a silver bowl for a beagle sitting quietly under a patron's table. The woman at whose feet the dog sat glared at the waiter and warned him, "Pas de vin blanc," no white wine for my dog. He was still a puppy. Or maybe he only drank red wine.

- The lunch hour in America is thirty minutes long. People work through their lunch hour. In France the lunch hour is two hours long. Nobody works. Even fully-automated, unmanned canal locks take a lunch hour. Trucks pull over on the highways. The sun does not move through the sky. Everything stops. Except lunch.

▪ Businesses in tourist areas in America make most of their annual income during the summer, when tourists are on vacation. Businesses in tourist areas in France are closed in August. Their employees are on vacation. And so are the owners. One August, we found a boulangerie in Saint Leger-sur-Dheune, in Burgundy, that was not closed for August vacation. I was excited until I saw a sign on the door. It was closed for the month because the owners had just had a baby, Justine. Her weight and height were on the "ferme" sign.

▪ When taking a Sunday after-lunch promenade in America, unlike in France, it is not necessary to offer a barely perceptible nod to every couple walking in the opposite direction, nor to mutter a formal "monsieur-dame." In France, this acknowledgement is mandatory. Nonetheless, the French expect their privacy to be respected, even in public, and they respect yours. In a gite – a sort of bed-and-breakfast – at which we stayed, the couple at the next table at breakfast chatted in imperceptible whispers. They were polite. Or talking about us. We couldn't hear them. Sandra was frustrated. Table eavesdropping is part of her French learning process.

▪ It is unlikely in America that the butcher shop walls will be covered with gold ribbons won by cows, the parts of whom are displayed in the butcher's cases. It is even less likely the cow's actual head will be in the case, next to the tenderloin. And even if your American butcher made his own sausage it is unlikely that he shot the sanglier – wild boar – himself. It is unlikely you will be able to find a butcher shop in your home town. Meat comes from the supermarket. In plastic. With an eat-by-date label.

▪ Bread . . . No, no, no. I crossed "bread" off the America-list. There is nothing to compare. You can't compare French bakeries with American bakeries because American bakeries exist in only one place: our memories. I can't think of a bakery within biking distance of our Ipswich home. A cloud of doom wallowed over me when our daughter Nicole attempted to console me about missing my daily morning pain au chocolate by saying that "at least you'll have Marty's Donutland," Ipswich's version of Dunkin Donuts. That distressing alternative almost led to cancellation of our airline tickets. Our first day home Sandra bought me a baguette at the supermarket. It was wrapped in plastic (PLASTIC!!). The bread and the wrapper had similar tastes. And textures. I couldn't finish it. And there were no swans swimming nearby to toss the remnants to.

So much for lists. We backed our bags, leaving clothing on the boat so we could stuff our bags with seventeen bottles of wine. I know Americans are warned that they are strictly forbidden to enter the country with more than two bottles of alcohol, but a friendly Customs agent once confessed to us that the duty on each additional bottle is just 75 cents and unless the duty exceeds ten dollars they don't bother with it.

Then, after a last minute visit to a fromagerie in Dijon and a conversation there with Madame left me with about ten pounds of carefully triple-wrapped, vacuum-sealed unpasteurized cheeses, I left all my shoes on the barge and replaced them with cheese.

Being an attorney, I did my research before importing any French cheese to the U.S.. An alphabet soup of federal agencies stood between me in France with stinky cheese and me in Ipswich with the same cheese. The CBP (Customs and Border Protection Service) of the DHS (Department of Homeland Security) enforces FIMA (the Federal Import Milk Act of 1927, Public Law 69-625, codified as 21 U.S.C. 141-149) as implemented by the regulations of APHIS (the Animal and Plant Health Inspection Service) of the USDA (U.S. Department of Agriculture), which prohibit the import of most (especially soft) unpasteurized CHEESE (cheese). Interestingly, while slamming the door on my favorite French cheeses these regulations rigorously allow only one fly per can of milk. See, USDA Compliance Policy Guide Sec. 527.200, titled Cheese & Cheese Products – Adulteration with Filth (you would think the Food and Drug Administration could come up with a less repulsive title for its food purity rules). While the nutritional value of flies appears to be a matter of debate at the Food and Drug Administration, unpasteurized milk products are viewed as terrorist tools.

As it turns out, I can more easily buy a semiautomatic version of an AK47 assault rifle in the U.S. than I can buy the same unpasteurized Brie de Meaux they sell at the fromage counter at every Intermarché grocery store in France.

Nonetheless, fresh from successfully thumbing our noses at the dread German Wasserpolice on the Rhine River, I chose to sneer at the American Homeland Security Gestapo by running raw dairy past their hyper vigilant snouts. I filled my duffel bag with kilograms of unpasteurized Epoisses de Bourgogne, 24-month old Comte from the Jura, triple cream Brillat-Savarin ("triple" – by French law – means the fat content is at least 75 percent, mon dieu!), and of course, Brie de Meaux, Emperor Charlemagne's favorite cheese in the Tenth Century. I was a tad apprehensive arriving at Boston's Logan Airport and steeled myself to confront the fiercest defense America could mount against the Threat of Worldwide Dairy Terror. So what is The Number One Global Power's first line of defense, you may ask?

A cutesy wootsy beagle.

My bags were approached by a beagle evidently highly trained to detect explosives. Or maybe narcotics. Or possibly unhygienic tiny terrorist elves. But not to sniff out raw cheeses. The puppy, who I hope was named Snoopy, failed to react to my pungent luggage. I barely came to a full stop before whisking past the electrified barbed wire fences and ion beam security devices to breathe the free air – cough, cough – of Boston, dragging my bagful of clandestine cholesterol.

I risked imprisonment to smuggle my Brie de Meaux past the none-too-alert beagle. Yes, Title 21, Chapter 4, Subchapter IV, Section 145 of the Import Milk Act warns that "any person who knowingly violates any provision of this subchapter shall, in addition to all other penalties prescribed by law, be punished by a fine of not less than $50 nor more than $2,000, or by imprisonment for not more than one year, or by both such fine and imprisonment." I pictured myself in prison stripes, squatting in my cell, explaining to my father-raper cellmate that I was doing hard time for soft cheese. Arriving home, I was surprised to find some of these same cheeses are sold in our local cheese shop. It turns out French cheesemakers clone for-export-only pasteurized – or, heaven forbid, irradiated – versions of their top-selling cheeses in a manner that satisfies American regulatory bureaucrats, even if they don't taste anything like their French namesakes.

Readjusting to stationary life in America would take some time. But I had until next Spring.

Learning the ropes, of the barge and of France

Four summers, and one winter, on the barge in France leads to some random observations:

Observation 1 - John Travolta was correct when he said the French know how to live life. Perhaps it's because we were in the countryside – life in Paris may be more like living in New York, or Boston – but the people we interacted with every day lived slower, fuller lives than we are used to at home. It was like living in 1952. Take Sundays, most any Sunday, even cold rainy Sundays. Sunday lunch takes hours and hours. You sit at a long table jammed with people, old people, young people, children, a dog or two. Course after course is served. Bottle after bottle is poured. It seems chaotic but follows a pattern and a pace that has been repeated for centuries. Sunday lunch ends with a promenade, a walk, for us that winter a walk along the River Saone, a walk with hundreds of other people, elderly couples with canes and walkers, elderly couples on bicycles, young families with children on bikes with training wheels, lovers stopping every three steps to kiss while people walk past them on both sides, old women walking tiny dogs on short leashes, young men with large dogs, unleashed, magnetically attached to their heels, men with three-piece suits wearing berets, teenagers dressed in full "NYC" regalia – baseball caps, high school jackets, long baggy shorts, all plastered with random English words – and a couple of Americans taking in the scene, greeting and being greeted with "monsieur-dame" by every couple they pass.

Observation B - But the winter wasn't all foie gras and fabulous friends. Some days, winter days, were cold and dreary. An 87-year-old former commercial boat does not hum like a factory fresh Mercedes. HOOP DOET LEVEN is more like a moderately healthy but increasingly aging old man. Its stomach rumbles and it isn't as agile as in younger days. Strange noises are heard in the middle of the night, elderly iron creaking and, hopefully, not cracking. Pumps that don't pump. Hoses and clamps sagging, losing their grips, just saying no. The toilet moans. Drips drop. It rains inside the bedroom as an evening's exhalations condense on cold iron ceilings.

Most every day has a list, a shopping list and a fix-it list.

Observation 3 - Giving each other space while living in a confined space was vital. This experience was a shared one, learning to live in France, learning to live on a boat, learning to handle the boat together as a crew. We have our assigned and/or default roles, I nurse the boat's systems, Sandra is our ambassador to the French. Yet so much of the vast amount of effort it takes to make this whole endeavor work is joint effort, planning our routes, operating the boat, and the sheer physical labor of living without cars. We came to depend on each other's skills and competency. The counterpoint is that we recognized we were each going to have a bad day from time to time and we each needed to get away, physically and emotionally, once in a while.

Sandra escaped into France. A barge neighbor, a retired Royal Navy officer, devoted large portions of the winter to tutoring me in the world of rugby - watching it on TV, not actually playing the game - an activity that involved equal amounts of beer and single malt scotch.

Observation V - Accommodating to living so closely with one another combined with accommodating to living in France. And the three fundamental rules of French life:

Rule Number One is that there is a strict rule for every interaction between people, with the government and with commerce.

Rule Number Two is that absolutely no exception can ever, under any circumstances be made to Rule Number One.

Rule Number Three is that, but of course, if one chooses to do so, an exception to Rule Number Two can be made but only just this one time. Rule Number Three is the oil that lubricates French life. Without Rule Number Three you might as well be living in the Soviet Union. Or Germany.

For example, not being European Union citizens, we were allowed to remain in France for more than a three month tourist visit by the granting of a carte de sejour, a one-year residency permit. The procedure for applying for the carte de sejour was Byzantine. We had to deliver a collection of forms in person at the French consulate in Boston, before ever setting off for France. After an interview there, we received full-page holographic stamps in our passports. Had we waited until we'd arrived in France to begin that process, we would have been sent back to Boston to apply. Immediately after arriving in France we had to submit the exact same forms again and, following X-rays, an eye examination - the most difficult part of which was remembering the names of the letters in French: H is "osh," I is "ee," E is "air," Z is "zed" - a non-physical physical examination, which, for me consisted in toto of answering two questions: are you healthy and so, are you marrying a French woman, and another personal interview, our passports were again holographically stamped with one-year residency permits on the page following the original one.

A year later, we dreaded the renewal process at the local marie, the Auxonne town hall. Fortunately, this interview was an exercise of Rule Number Three. Our medical insurance certification, proof that we had the mandatory coverage to pay to ship our remains out of France should we die here, so as not to despoil French soil with our corpses (which apparently is allowed only if you die rescuing France from the Germans), had been mailed to our son in New Hampshire, our token mailing address. He'd scanned the certification and emailed a copy to us. But you absolutely must present the original, we were told at the marie. The copy is unacceptable. Sandra smiled and chatted about our vacation on the Cote d'Azur, all in her best French. She pointed out that the clerk's boots were unlaced and prayed she would not trip on them. The woman smiled and – voila – with a swipe of her Rule Number Three rubber stamp, the copy became acceptable.

French banks, however, are bastions of Rules Number One and Two. Banks here don't hand out toasters and gift certificates to new customers. No, French banks are more like Mr. Grumpy's house on Halloween night, porch lights are turned off and the house dark so trick or treaters will be lured into believing nobody is home. Trying to deposit a check to your bank account makes you feel as if you are disposing of your collection of doggie poop bags. And don't ask for change. They don't have any, at least not today. The ATM may dispense fifty-euro notes, but no bank teller can change them to any size bill that any French store keeper will accept. We have a phone number that supposedly rings through to our special personal bank representative at the HSBC branch on the Avenue des Champs-Élysées in Paris. He will solve any problem we might have, in English, the bank promised us. When I dialed his number a recording told me, in French, it was no longer in service.

Observation 6 - When arriving any place, the boulangerie, a doctor's waiting room, boarding a train, a work place, you must greet everybody present in the proper manner, ranging from a nod through a bonjour to a handshake to un bisou, a kiss on one, two or three cheeks, the correct number depending on who, where, when and, possibly the phase of the moon. Leaving requires at least an au revoir. Leaving your table at a restaurant, you say goodbye to everybody you pass at every table. This rule can be seen in action when you observe somebody arriving at work. Every coworker must be greeted, every hand must be shaken. By every employee. On a large enough job site – and I've watched at construction sites – saying good morning to your coworkers takes almost until lunch, just about when you have to begin your goodbyes. La Monde reported an American executive complaining about French workers, "They have one hour for their breaks and lunch, talk for three and work for three." The workers' response, "That's the French way."

Observation VII - Food, everything you've heard about French food is true. In Paris we dropped in at the shop of master chocolate maker Patrick Roger. He is one of the few chocolatiers to receive the title of Meilleur Ouvrier de France ("Best Craftsmen of France"), a government competition to anoint the masters of various trades, from locksmithing to hair styling to day care working to – yes, chocolate making. (Just imagine, for a moment, the pyrotechnics that would be ignited if President Obama proposed that the government select the best chocolate maker, or plumber, in the United States.) Entering the competition costs around 50,000 euros. Few people win their first try. He did. After tasting a saffron and basil chocolate he'd made, Snickers bars are a thing of the past.

At the other extreme, snapping the tip off a baguette (the single mouthful one is permitted – another Rule Number One – to eat on the street is called the "crouton") baked within the half hour and still warm, from almost any local boulangerie is as mouth satisfying as food can be. A baba au rhum dessert at a buchon – a small, working persons' lunch restaurant – in Lyon, which is acknowledged as the food capital of France, meaning, of the entire Universe, was simply a cake and a bottle of sweetened rum you poured over the cake.

Sure, food is serious business pretty much everywhere. But the difference between everyday food in France and in the States, though, is that the concepts of supersizing, bottomless coffee cups and enough food to require a take-home bag, concepts that have positive connotations at home, are replaced in France with a struggle toward excellence, toward quality, tradition, simply toward fineness. Appreciation for good food is taught in school, and at home. You see two butcher shops side by side, but one has a line out to the sidewalk, the other is empty. It will soon be closed. People search for quality, rather than quantity, in their food.

One compromise to living on a boat, especially during chilly months, was that at least once a month we booked a hotel room. With a bath tub. Un chambre avec un salle de bain avec bain, we learned to request. A secondary benefit of this practice was that we got to watch French television in the hotel room. (The barge has a TV, one we bought in our first week on board, but none of the plug-in antennas we've bought brings in a signal and our satellite dish hasn't worked since I stayed up all night to watch Obama's reelection – obviously a Republican device – so we only use the TV to watch DVDs and video cassettes). French TV is mostly sharply dressed men and women discussing events in Mali or Marseilles, French soap operas, some dubbed American shows (The Simpsons seems to be on the air constantly, how French), and children's cartoons. And there was a lesson in French culture. Our favorite cartoon was about a collection of vegetables who ran a pizza shop and spoke in the squeaky voices of cartoon characters. They mostly chattered back and forth, a cute young carrot girl and a vaguely human boy who was some sort of generic veggie. A customer arrived and ordered a Special Pizza. Oh, they were so excited. Then disaster struck. Monsieur Evil - a quasi tomato - broke in and stole all the Special Pizza Sauce. What would they do? The veggie boy leapt in the air and spun ferociously as the music reached a crescendo. In the best tradition of action heroes worldwide, in the steps of mild mannered Clark Kent transforming into Superman, of Mr. Mellow Bruce Wayne becoming bold Batman, veggie waiter boy stopped rotating and emerged as . . . Super Server. Yes, carrot girl screamed in awe, Super Server, Super Server you are here to save us. All in French, of course.

Now, can there be another country on the planet where Evil is banished by the intervention of the World's Best Waiter? Where the Waiter is the action hero, not the Hero's nerdly alter ego? Is there the slightest possibility American children would rush out to buy action figures of a waiter? Yet here we were in prime after-school television time watching the les Aventures de Super Serveur. How did he save the day, you may ask. Well, Mr. Evil, being a tomato turned bad, was trying to force carrot girl to cover her Special Pizza with ketchup. No, never, a thousand times no, she cried, just as Little Nell spurned Snidely Whiplash until she was rescued by Dudley Do-Right of the Canadian Mounties. Super Serveur flew out the window and returned in moments with armloads of dew-covered fresh tomatoes and pockets filled with herbs and spices. The Super Special Pizza was truly super special, the restaurant was saved and carrot girl's heart throbbed for Super Server.

How French is that? But it was only that day's nugget of Frenchness.

It went on and on. That first year was a gift we gave to ourselves. But it happened only because we consciously chose to make it happen and went through intensive efforts to bring it about. Back in lawyering days, negotiations and mediations were a large part of my litigation repertoire. One rule of negotiating was to consider your BATNA, your Best Alternative to a Negotiated Agreement, meaning, if you fail to reach an agreement, what happens next and will that be better or worse for you than a compromise would have been.

I think about our BATNA to this time in France. How would these years been had we stayed home. And what would the next year be like if we called quits to this adventure? Looked at that way, the choice was simple. France – sometimes cold, sometimes dreary, sometimes frustrating, sometime just simply exhausting – gave us a life more stimulating, more fulfilling, more exciting than remaining at home would have. Moments of doubt were few and effervescent. The counterpoint to this was our frustration when friends at home would say they were living vicariously through us. That is more responsibility than we wanted. Go ahead and rely on us as pathfinders, as scouts, but please don't live vicariously through us. As Jerry Rubin, my Yippee leader, told us in the 1960s, "do it" – not necessarily a barge in France, but whatever blows your own whistle – for yourself.

Crouching in a box

We're deep into planning our fifth French summer on Hoop Doet Leven. Tucked in a corner of the bedroom closet is a cardboard box. Into that box gets tossed stuff that will be going to France with us next Spring. The boat insurance renewal forms. A Costco-sized potpourri of resealable plastic bags because if there is one thing the U.S. of A. does right it is manufacturing rugged, multi-usable resealable plastic bags. Same goes for disposable foam paint brushes. I bought a 40-pack of them. I give them as gifts to other bargees.

And, most important of all, that box holds the keys to the barge.

France, and Hoop Doet Leven, changed us. Changed, without question, for the better. Sandra and I led busy, productive lives before retirement. But in many ways they were separate lives. Different jobs. Different careers. Different work families. Different hobbies. Competing hobbies. Sailing and gardening have little in common, except for demands on warm weather time. We'd had long, anxious discussions about what we would be doing after we both retired.

Sailing around the world was obviously an unshared dream. Once I recognized that, the sailboat was turned around and headed back toward home. Settling into our nest at home was also not shared. A youth spent as a golf caddy created a lifelong antipathy to whacking a little white ball around fancy pastures as a way to spend my golden years.

One thing was clear, though. An encounter with cancer - non-Hodgkin's lymphoma - in my late forties opened my eyes to the concept of if there is something you want to do before you die, better do it soon, before you die.

We were fortunate in coming up with a compromise, the whole "buy an old barge and cruise the French canals" business, a compromise that would not have been my first choice — driving a motorboat up and down a ditch didn't strike me as nearly boatie enough — and wouldn't have been Sandra's either. Living on boats for more than an afternoon exceeded her quota. But it was a compromise and we both committed to it.

And it worked. A lifetime navigating sailboats along oceans and rocky shores supplied me with almost no skills that contributed to driving a 65-ton steel barge through skinny canals and up and down locks. Mastering new skills was exciting. Rewarding. And, in the long run, satisfying.

For Sandra, whose philosophy is that there is no reason to do something 100 percent when you can do it 200 percent, learning French, and about the French, was a challenge that still takes up hours of her days. And a boat that is never more than a few yards from land isn't too boatie for her to tolerate.

Ultimately, what made this barge experience so rewarding was that in retirement we were sharing our experiences, following the same path, rather than just meeting each evening after going our separate ways all day. Success required both of us to rely on each other's skills and knowledge. We were operating as a team.

We don't know how long we'll stay on Hoop Doet Leven. The original plan was to give it a two-year commitment. We'd purposefully shopped for a boat we thought would be easy to sell if things didn't work out. Two months into France we agreed we were hooked, that this lifestyle worked for us and that we'd keep doing it as long as we could.

Sure, learning to operate a 90-year-old boat in a foreign country isn't everybody's dream. But the barge is just a vehicle for our dream. One of hundreds of conceivable vehicles for hundreds of conceivable dreams.

The trick was in fashioning the dream. The real trick was then to go ahead and hop onto the vehicle for realizing that dream.

We've spent four summers, and one winter, on the boat in France. Maneuvered through 1,242 locks. I keep count in the logbook. Traveled through just one corner of France so far. We are the only creatures in nature to migrate east and west every year, rather than north and south. We spend our winters preparing for the next summer.

And once in a while, when I am home alone, I walk into the bedroom closet and scrunch down in the cardboard box we mentally labeled as the place to put items that absolutely, positively must return to France next year.

About the author

Harvey Schwartz is a retired Boston civil rights attorney. Although he argued two cases before the United States Supreme Court, he is perhaps best known in Massachusetts for successfully overturning the state's ban on tattooing. He argued that tattoos are art and that as artistic speech, the right to tattoo is protected by the First Amendment of the United States Constitution. As a reward, he was declared the Massachusetts Tattoo Artists Association Mass Ink Man of the Year. As punishment, however, both his sons' are encrusted with tattoos.

In 2011, Mr. Schwartz and his wife, Sandra Hamilton, purchased Hoop Doet Leven, a 21 meter (70 foot) former commercial canal barge built in the Netherlands in 1926. They lived on Hoop Doet Leven in France for twenty months and have spent every summer since then cruising the French canals and rivers, primarily in northeastern and central France.

Mr. Schwartz also wrote a novel, The Reluctant Terrorist, presenting a plausibly terrifying depiction of events similar to the Holocaust happening in the United States. That book is available from Amazon in paper and electronically.

When not in France, Harvey and Sandra live in Ipswich, Massachusetts. He operates Marshview Boatworks, building small wood rowing and paddling boats.

They maintain a blog about their travels at www.onabargeinfrance.com.

Made in the USA
Monee, IL
01 May 2021